SPRING SOWING

SPRING SOWING

by

MICHAEL HOME

Illustrated by

HELLMUTH WEISSENBORN

METHUEN & CO. LTD. LONDON
36 Essex Street, Strand, W.C.2

First published in 1946

PRINTED IN GREAT BRITAIN

FOR
MY MOTHER
ON HER 83RD BIRTHDAY

TO THE READER

so many readers of *Autumn Fields* have asked for a continuation of its recollections of Heathley and Breckland, that it would be ingratitude to refuse. The publishers, unmindful of Goldsmith's condemnation of making into a series a work that has achieved some measure of popularity, have asked for a continuation. It was a gratifying proposal, however dubious I may be of my ability to make a successor that will be other than something of an anti-climax.

In *Autumn Fields* the author was the narrator and things were seen against his background and through his eyes. *Spring Sowing*—as its title implies—is more nearly an autobiography even if it never quite becomes one. I could wish that it were even less. The things that matter are still a way of life and a countryside that have almost gone, and, except as their narrator or remembrancer, the author is of small account.

In *Spring Sowing* we are back again at fifty years ago, but whereas *Autumn Fields* was static, its continuation must necessarily move, though little beyond a further ten years. But those bounds are not guaranteed. Like its predecessor it will meander, ramble and go off at queer tangents. As was said, it is a poor country lane that has no attractive by-path and even youth is entitled to anticipate a future.

To avoid repetition the assumption must be made that the reader of *Spring Sowing* has read *Autumn Fields*. But if he has not, then I do not think a possible pleasure will be spoiled. If occasionally, however, there are references for the sake of clarity to what is already known, perhaps these will be pardoned. The maps of Heathley and the surrounding Brecklands are printed as end-papers.

M. H.

May 1945

CONTENTS

Chapter I

BRIEF HISTORY

YOU will not, I trust, be alarmed at the heading of this first chapter, even if the mention of brevity has failed to reassure you. Fifty years ago, when John Balfour lent me one by one the novels of Scott, I ventured to point out to him that nothing ever happened till one had read an inordinately long first chapter, and I still remember the lecture he gave me. You can imagine what it was: the value of a sure background and the necessity for placing isolated events in their proper contexts. All that remains perfectly true, but let me put it another way.

When a Scottish-Nationalist Member towards the end of the last Parliament refused to accept the services of sponsors, the House was divided in its attitude. It is symptomatic of the exigent thinking and commercialization of this age of rapidly urbanizing villages and ever new suburbias, that some eighty Members should have considered that the custom itself should be abrogated. The then Prime Minister thought otherwise. The House, he said, should cling tenaciously to its ancient customs and procedure if only because those things were the very framework of its dignity and the breath of its being.

Those reasons seem to me to apply with some cogency to our ancient English villages, for history, custom and tradition lend them a dignity, though history and continuity be invisible or unobserved. But permit me first to explain what I mean by a village. The explanation is an obstinate and even pig-headed one of my own, and perhaps a negative definition is as good as any. What I do not mean, then, is what I have called an urbanized village: one of those Sussex villages, for instance, the haunt of week-enders and whose larger houses are occupied by retired members of the Services or even authors like myself, whose exploitation is a rural industry. What I mean is a village like that in which my ancestors have a recorded history of hundreds of years: a village still remote and untouched by commercialism, with a native population that speaks its dialect and whose roots run deep.

In such a village, then, the placing of a church is still seen to have been not wholly by chance, or the clustering of houses about a church or manor. Even in its central open space one can discern something of history. Mills may have almost disappeared, but a ruin may remain on some windy site. Old customs may have gone or remain in forms that are deeply disguised, but for those to whom the past still has value there are documents that are accessible, even if they are only parish registers. Many a townsman would be surprised to learn that there are villages whose recorded history is more ample and more complete than that of many towns.

Take the remote village of Heathley that lies on the edge of the great heaths and brecklands of south-west Norfolk. Once it was a flourishing little township, but now it is little more than a hamlet. Yet it has a recorded history of a thousand years, and in those years underwent the changes of growth, decline and growth in many cycles. Of the last of those changes I was myself a part.

Over fifty years ago, after some years with an aunt who had intended to adopt me, I returned to that little Norfolk village at the age of eight, and was at once absorbed into its life. Even then it was, if unknowingly, in the process of what may be a final decay, though still possessed of a certain communal life and an evanescent prosperity that depended ironically enough on the prime cause of its death—the Game Laws. To-day it is moribund. The last news that has reached me is tragical enough, for it has even ceased to have a vicar and a vicarage, and its rare church services are taken by a neighbouring incumbent. But fifty years ago the signs of decay were there, if only like the last hectic flush on the face of a consumptive. Heathley was a farming village with no crafts or industries. It lived or died by the land, and yet its outlying fields on which in my father's boyhood the stacks stood thick as the fingers of a hand, I saw only when devoured by the onward surge of bracken and the rabbit. Those nearer fields where fifty years ago I raked and mowed and served a thatcher are now covered with the young plantations of the Forestry Commission, and arable land remains only to the east. The beauty of new-turned earth, and young corn, and the poignant melancholy of an autumn stubble are now obscured by the impersonal rigidity of innumerable trees, unreal and unnatural as those toy spruces that my aunt bought for me as a child to flank the entrance to a Noah's Ark. Where forty men once worked, one will now suffice, and what the ultimate harvest will be is beyond my imagining, unless it be pit-props for yet another war.

The death of an individual, save in martrydom or war, is rarely a triumph. If few deaths are so obscure as to be without some personal tragedy, then the death of a village must be a tragedy indeed. One value of history, we are told, is that it teaches the errors of the past, but once a village is dead there is nothing I know of in history to effect a resurrection. All that can be done is to record the fact for the benefit of history, and maybe, if curiously minded, to state the cause of death. And there the implied metaphor breaks down, for while judgment may be pronounced on the crime, the killer is beyond justice. Indeed, by some satanic irony, we are ourselves the ultimate criminals, as in that matter of the years between the last two wars.

But to revert to the village of Heathley. The map shows it as it was fifty years ago. It lay, and still lies, open to the east, with the bracken and the rabbit, and both in a way protected by the Game Laws, encroaching from south and west and north. Once it was Heathley Magna and had a Heathley Parva. Little Heathley, now surviving only in name, lay between the main village and the Illboro boundary. But I am not going to bore you with a long history of the two Heathleys, though there is material enough for a score of pages. And, to be frank, I am no archaeologist, and when I was confronted with the records I had to use the service of an interpreter for the much that I failed to understand: details of manorial rights, for instance, and customs and privileges with a manor, with such terms as leet fees, liberty of free warren, view of frankpledge, assizes of ale and bread, or the dowering of women with a moiety of a copyhold. But shorn of such ancient or antiquated terms, here is very briefly the history of the two Heathleys.

My father, a Radical of Radicals and a Ranter of Ranters, whose roots were centuries deep in Heathley soil, was deeply concerned with the rights of the labouring man. My mother was a London woman, more gently nurtured and of keener inward perceptions, and it was when she expressed some distaste for local politics or spoke a good word for parson or squire that my father would exclaim, or roar, 'Church and State! That's what you are, Mrs. Home. Church and State!' To him those were the eternal and arch enemies, and I mention the fact because in this brief history Church and State are intertwined.

Great Heathley was always one manor and in the time of Edward the Confessor it belonged to a certain Edric. After the Conquest it fell to Roger Bigod, and he parted with it to the Albanys and they sold it to the Montchensys. Henry III gave to Dionise de Montchensy a charter for a fair and market to be held in Great Heathley every Friday, thus conferring much of the status of a town. She had freedom of game throughout all her manor, and in that my father would have discerned a foreshadowing of Game Laws and a disregard and down-treading of tenants. But all the superior jurisdictions were in the hands of the Lord of Buckingham Castle, and I take it that Old Buckenham, some ten miles away, is meant. Under his authority the township had its assizes to try freedmen. But in the very year of that charter, Dionise apprehended a thief in Heathley and hanged him out of hand, and for that she was brought to account before the king's sheriff.

Just short of the Peddar's Way where the boundaries of Heathley, Wortley, and Topleigh meet, there is a slight rise of ground known as Gallows Hill. But I doubt if it was there that the thief was hanged. Either it was on the open space of the township, known to us as the Mound, or within the precincts of the manor itself. Where that house stood is a mystery, but there must have been a very great house with many buildings to lodge the lord or his steward. For my own part I am fairly sure that that great house stood in what is now a wood, still enclosed by a moat, on a meadow along the Larford Road known as Moat Meadow, and opposite the farm still known as Moat Farm. It is a fair site on rich flat land, and I have found traces of what I believe to have been a tilting ground. In my younger days when I might have made researches there, such research was impossible. That wood, like every other in the parish, was sacred to the pheasant or its eggs. But I did explore it surreptitiously as a boy, and it was there that I found the descendants of cob nuts, and strange sterile fruit trees among the tangled undergrowth. And though, as I said, I am no archaeologist, yet it seems to me that it is easy to explain why that manor did not stand near the church, since the church at the time of its building was the property of the Priors of Ouseland.

After Dionise de Montchensy the manor changed hands every few years, for those were turbulent and unstable times. The Earls of Pembroke had it, and the de Greys of Ruthyn, and the Nevills and Beauchamps, all of them great names. Heathley Mere, now a part of Cranberry, is mentioned as being separate water of the lords of the manor. It was two hundred and eighty acres in extent and the lord had a fish-house there. In later times much of this mere was reclaimed by the parish, only to have it filched under the Enclosure Acts. In 1654 it is recorded that the township of Great Heathley held certain lands of the manor of Walsingham, and a glance at the map will show that the ancient Peddar's Way ran straight as a taut line from the great abbey of Walsingham along the western boundary of Heathley to the still greater Abbey of St. Edmund, twenty miles to the south. But a more noteworthy fact is this, that in that same year the two Heathleys were assessed £628 6s. 8d. to the King's Tax, a notable sum for those times and showing the prosperity of a thriving community.

The manor continued to change hands. The Kedlingtons seem to have held it the longest and it is their memorials that are still to be found in the church. Then the Ryleys acquired it, and it was Philip Ryley who, in about 1720, built what is described as a 'neat brick house'. That is the present Hall, an early Georgian building with a huge walled garden. It faces a fair-sized park with a fine vista and many noble trees. The lord of the manor now owned the advowson, which may explain the site and the fact that a private path connects with the church. Ryley's successors made a private road which connects with the Wortley Road, and they laid out the woods and made a fish-pond. Over a hundred years later it came into the possession of another legal family, the Finches, who held it till about 1930 when the whole estate was broken up and sold to a firm of speculators, the Forestry Commission acquiring all lands deemed suitable for their plantings. During all my boyhood and youth the Hall was in the occupation of a shooting tenant. He enlarged the Hall and added, among other things, a billiard-room.

So much for what might be called the State. The church, dedicated to the Trinity, was a rectory, appended to the manor. Then in 1227 Warene de Montchensy gave the living to Richard, the Prior of the monks of Ouseland, and until the Dissolution of the Monasteries the priors presented various monks as vicars. All their names are recorded, and most were local men, as Robert of Brandon, Robert Stugg of Ouseland, William Sparescho of Ixworth, and Robert Fenn of Rushworth.

After the Dissolution the advowson of the vicarage went with the abbey of Ouseland and all its revenues to Thomas, Duke of Norfolk, and Heathley's first vicar under the New Dispensation was a Thomas Halstede. But the Duke soon parted with his Breckland properties, and maybe because he parted with his head, and there followed a new series of changes of ownership. Then finally Heathley was bought, manor, advowson and all, by the Jermyns. The names of all the vicars had continued to be consistently recorded, and Blomefield (c. 1800) gave the value of the living as about four hundred pounds. He added that the church had lost its original tower, the ruins of which lay at the west end.

Of all those names recorded as in any way connected with Heathley Church, there is only one that interests me personally. It is typical, too, of the vicissitudes that overcame both the Homes and the Poleys. I never had the honour of a genuine nickname, though my sisters would often try to annoy me by calling me Poley, for it was after a distant relative, the last of the Poleys that I was named. In 1532 it is recorded that Robert Poley was buried in the churchyard and left certain funds 'to find and kepe a light before our Lady of Pitye with five prickett candells of wax to burn in the church of Heathley in tyme of divyne service for ever'. But beyond the name, I inherited nothing from that last of the Poleys, unless in some strange way it was my love of music, for he was a teacher of music and an organist, and that although he was blind.

So much for best part of a thousand years of Heathley history. My father would savagely have noted that whereas the lords of the manor were all known and the long line of rectors and vicars, nothing was said of the common man except perhaps by implication. His rise from serf and villein to freedman and possibly tenant farmer can be read with that of his contemporaries in Trevelyan. But that Heathley was a place of importance cannot be denied. Its natural position made it so, for it lay midway, and on the pilgrim road, between two of the greatest abbeys in England, and at the gateway from the vast hinterlands of heath to the great city of Norwich. Its medieval population of two hundred may not sound much, but all England then had only a matter of five millions. In Tudor times it grew rapidly, and before the Hungry Forties its population was about eight hundred. Then it declined but rose to some five hundred in the 'eighties, and that was when I first knew it. I doubt if its population at this moment is two hundred.

To supplement its recorded history with imagination would be futile. Maybe its bowmen fought at Crécy and Agincourt, and maybe they did not. Most certainly they profited by plagues and the Black Death to improve their lot, and I like to imagine that some fought against oppression with Kett, the Wymondham tanner, though none, I hope, was hanged with Kett when Warwick crushed that brief rebellion. That some men of Heathley fought with Cromwell seems fairly certain. Even in Elizabeth's time there was a Puritan element, and the Homes were part of it.

There remains Little Heathley. In the Confessor's time it belonged to a certain Aelwine and after the Conquest it, too, fell to Roger Bigod. At that time the Priory of Ouseland was founded and Roger at once gave the church of St. Mary at Little Heathley and its tithes to the new foundation. Later, you may remember they received a similar gift from Warene de Montchensy of the church of Great Heathley. Thereafter only one vicar was needed to serve the two parishes, and for that reason the church was allowed to fall into disrepair and in a very few years it was a ruin. No trace, even of its site, remains.

As for the manor, that passed through various hands, but after the Dissolution of the Monasteries it fell into the hands of the King. Finally one of the Jermyn family bought it and

joined it to the manor of Great Heathley. In 1616 there were
five copyhold holdings whose rents were the considerable sum
of £31 12s. 0d., and besides two other tenements, there was a
sheepwalk. In 1737 there were still two farms there. When I
first knew it fifty years ago there was only the one farm. Even
the manor-house built by William Jermyn had gone and there
was in its place an early Victorian house known as Little
Heathley Hall. Most of the ancient arable land had fallen out
of cultivation and the low meadows towards the river were
choked with rushes and sedge. The heath had swallowed
much of it to the south-west, and its one road across the small
stream of Illboro was only a rutted track. Little Heathley, as
I said, has ceased to exist except in name and that a name of
convenience. Heathley itself is never Great Heathley, except
in official descriptions, and when we speak of Heathley,
Little Heathley, if thought of at all, is included.

So much for what might be called ancient history. Now,
perhaps, I may be permitted to carry on that history to the
period of this book.

Fifty years ago Squire Finch lived at Little Heathley Hall.
The estate had long ceased to pay its way and so the Hall,
together with the Hill Farm, was let to Green, known by
courtesy or lip-serving as Squire Green. He was a member of
a firm of international bankers; a red-faced, pompous, blustering man unversed in country history and ways. Like Dionise
de Montchensy he had the right of free-warren, though in his
case it was not exactly free, for he must have paid a considerable
sum for the shooting rights and tenancies. Under him
Heathley became one of the finest shoots in all England.
Hundreds of pheasants were anually reared each spring and
each early summer transferred to rides in the woods and there
fed. When that artificial feeding ceased, the birds lived on the
cornfields of the tenant farmers. Then in winter there would
be shooting parties at the Hall, with as many as a thousand
head killed in a day, and every spare village man and boy
lending a hand as brushers[1] or on stop.[2] There were half a
dozen keepers, and Green built additional cottages for them
near outlying woods. As many men were in the Hall gardens,
with maids, footmen, butler, and housekeeper in the Hall
itself.

---

[1] Beaters.   [2] Men or boys at fixed posts to turn back the game.

John Pardon was vicar, and he had four grown-up children, of whom Maud, the younger of the two sisters, played the organ at church and assisted in the Sunday school with the daughter of Squire Finch. The Vicarage was a thriving place with its handsomely kept drive and gardens, its three maids and coachman and spare man.

In the village were no less than nine distinct farms. Hill Farm, as has been said, was farmed by Green with Wyatt as his steward, and for a time Wyatt was steward also at Little Heathley. West Farm, Moat Farm, and Cranberry were the only farms known by impersonal names, the others bore the names of their tenants. Boddy's farm lay towards the Brackford valley, though his house was in the village opposite Wilson's shop. Crawford's lay by the Shopleigh boundary and Kerridge's was between it and the village. Gaul's lay both sides of Vicarage Road, between the village and West Farm. Bullen's was at the far end of the Larford Road, with Moat Farm between it and the village. Half-way to Little Heathley lay the holding known as Lammas Meadows, and that we farmed.

In the village were three public-houses: the Lion, facing the Mound, the Crown in the Shopleigh Road and the Eagle at the corner where the Larford Road turns off from the school. There were four shops, the largest being the general stores of Robert Addis by the school. Almost next door was the post office store, and just short of the Vicarage Road was Wilson's shop. Just past the Vicarage Road was a bakery shop, and then there was the shop of William Cash just past Wilson's. Once it had been a tailor's, but now it sold little but the weekly papers.

The school, which served the outlying parts of neighbouring parishes, was in the hands of John Balfour and his wife, Mary. His house was the last along the Brackford Road and just beyond it was the Primitive Methodist chapel with its strong community of old-time Ranters. There were also two black-smiths, two shoemakers, two wheelwrights, and two bakers, and a London man was to set up a building business in the Larford Road, and make his money from work provided by Green. There was the great woodyard with its saw-mill, and there were estate carpenters and bricklayers. There was Potter, the constable, and a parish constable to lend aid. But there was no doctor nearer than the six miles to Harford or

Hareborough. There was no butcher, and when a man named
Tash did begin a business it speedily failed, for butcher's meat
was too dear, and all the year round the village lived on pork
and rabbits. Fish, chiefly bloaters and kippers, was hawked
round by our own Josh Till or by a man from Rockland,
which lies beyond Shopleigh. At Rockland, too, was the workhouse and infirmary to which the old and poor were eventually
taken.

Nineteen-twentieths of Heathley was, as we say, under the
Squire, but among the few cases of private ownership were the
inns, the shops, and the house in which we lived. But Finch, in
any case, was a just man. It was only when a man depended for
his living on Green that he had to be wary of ways and words.
As for John Pardon, Methodist though I was and even at this
distance of fifty years, I still recall him with affection. To me,
as a boy, he was always a great man and something of a hero.
And he possessed an innate courtesy, never failing to acknowledge the raising of my cap, and to address me by my
Christian name.

The weekly market of Heathley had long since gone; in fact,
in 1654 it is mentioned as no longer existing. But the fair,
as granted in that charter to Dionise de Montchensy, remained
until my own time, though only as an annual fair in spring.
I remember my father asking us children at breakfast if we
knew what day it was, and then telling us—with something
of triumph and a laugh at his own recallings—that it was
Heathley Fair. Once I do remember a fair with swings and
roundabouts and stalls on the Mound, and the roads thronged
with people, but soon it dwindled to two stalls and finally to
one. That stall, in the shelter of the Lion wall, sold cockles
and whelks with oranges for the children.

In the days of my grandfather that annual fair used to last
for best part of a week, and my father just remembered the last
of it. Heathley Horn Fair was the name then given to it, and
from a very old custom surviving finally from the times when
strangers had to be strictly scrutinized. The last repository
of the horns, now vanished, was said to be the Lion, and the
horns themselves were a pair of huge ox-horns with the usual
hairy pad between. Before the actual opening of the fair the
horns would be fetched, and any stranger entering the village
had to undergo the rite of doshing[1] before being admitted to

[1] Norfolk *dosh*—dash.

the freedom of the fair. By doshing one implied that the man removed his headgear and butted the horns with his forehead as if he were a charging steer.

As to the rights and privileges of the householders of Heathley, only one remained in my boyhood. Most of the common and waste lands had been lost under the Enclosure Acts, but there remained a fair-sized common near the Brackford boundary where there was the right to cut furze for fuel. Grazing rights on that common were let by public tender and the monies returned in part at least to the poor of the parish, by gifts of winter coal.

So much for Heathley recorded history, though in part it may have been myself who have been the recorder. What follows may be called village history in the making, but my part will be merely to introduce you to people and places and to leave you largely to be your own recorder and assessor.

And once more a word of warning. Do not expect strict adherence to chronology, or, to be frank, adherence to anything. If a country road has its attractive side lanes, we shall leave the road and take those lanes. But those lanes may have paths and we may take them too and heaven knows where we shall ultimately emerge. But of one thing you may be sure. Though we may even go far afield to the towns of Breckland, sooner or later we shall return to Heathley and its people again.

Chapter II

THE VILLAGE

FOR me there are two Heathleys. There is the Heathley of my youth, and now as I close my eyes I can see each road, lane, and track as they then were. I can see each farm or cottage, and in many cases can see those perennial flowers that were the peculiar property of a house or cottage, or the plants that made splashes of colour in its little windows. I can see the occupants of each house, except for the younger children, and can recall their voices and differences of accent.

Then there is the other Heathley which for me has no existence—the Heathley of the last few years; a Heathley shorn of the abounding life of my boyhood, the land by which it lived disfigured, and the village itself overshadowed by those monstrous plantation growths, and its once shadowy lanes and roads denuded of their oaks. Even that most ancient and pleasant of all village sounds, the music of a forge, has ceased, and whether it be for lack of a blacksmith or for lack of work does not matter; the thing is that it has gone.

As I remember those things it seems that I should almost implore you to believe me when I say that Heathley, fifty years ago, was as lovely a village as I have ever known, and there is little of England that I have not seen. Its individual houses were not beautiful, and yet there was a beauty in their placing: the clustering of cottages round the Mound, for instance, and the trees on the Mound itself, so that by whichever road one passed there was always a light and a shadow through which one saw the cottages beyond. Since most of those cottages were thatched, as was the Lion itself that dominated them, and as each had its flowers or rose bushes straggling along its front, there was a series of colourful little vistas, and beyond them in the near distance the tops of oaks and elms.

But it was in its setting that the village had its particular loveliness. The heaths and brecks came round it like two fingers that have almost closed, and when I was a boy it was that opening towards the east that always seemed to me to be no real part of the village at all, and on my walks and bird-nesting expeditions I always shunned it, or if I had gone that way I would find myself cutting back to north or south. It was noteworthy, too, that the village itself in its walks always favoured the Wortley Road or the circuit round the Brackford Lane.

I wish I had the words to convey to you that utter remoteness of our western hinterland. No sooner did one pass West Farm than one had a choice of tracks that led through Cranberry to the great heaths of Topleigh and Tottley. The continuation of the Wortley Road past Gallows Hill led the same way. If one took the Illboro track there were the great heaths towards Rudgham and Ouseland, and even if one took the Hareborough Road and then one of the numerous lanes or tracks that led west, one could tramp for a day and more and still be in the brecklands. When on a Wednesday in my holidays I rode all day with Walter Addis in his cart, we were never out of the sight of brecks and heaths. As Punch jogged his way across the marled and flinty roads, the bracken brushed the wheels of the cart, and between the oases of hamlets would be the quiet and lonely miles. Between hamlet and hamlet it was rare to meet another cart or a living soul; indeed the only living things might be the crying peewits, aloof protected pheasants, or, if it were towards evening, the innumerable rabbits that rose at our approach and scattered to their sandy burrows as if the earth itself had moved in flight.

I wish, too, that I could convey to you the incredible beauty of that vast and lonely country. For all its quietude there was in it nothing forbidding. It had space and freedom and the friendliness of growing things. The heaths and brecks had their gentle undulations so that in lanes and tracks one never saw too far ahead. And then again there would be great sweeps of open country. And even there the miles of bracken or heather would have no monotony for they would be broken by ancient woods or clusters of gnarled pines, and mossy pools with their silver birches, or the oases of silver sand which were the burrows of the teeming rabbits. Above would be the open sky, and across the clear stretches it would be hard to tell where the faint blue of the horizon ended and that sky began. Then there were the meres, as varying as the heath itself. Ringmere and Langmere lay open while Fowlmere and Topleigh Watering were embowered in trees, though Topleigh was open on one side to the brecks. Everywhere was a prodigality of colour that somehow blended and harmonized, so that the golden flare of massed canker-weed seemed to merge into green bracken, and that again into the madders and lakes of the squat heather. And then when that colouring of the heaths seemed endless, one would suddenly be at a vast stretch of breck, the bare grey soil showing a sheen of dwarf flowers and always the silver-grey of the rabbit burrows.

But to the east, as I have said, we were open, though the best word seems to me to be 'different'. Now there were metalled roads and nothing else; the soil grew heavier and the land richer, and villages were no longer sparse. Beyond the villages lay the first towns, which even then meant modernity and markets. Even the air seemed different and there was an openness that gave a feeling of bareness now that the woodlands and the shady roads had gone. And yet in some curious way Heathley retained its own remoteness, as if it were loth to unlatch or even look through that still closed door. Harford, Attley, Ouseland, and Hareborough were more often places from which people came to us than places to which we went ourselves.

For the great bulk of our population were labouring men, and there was no leisure for sightseeing or visiting. The labourer and the tradesman worked six whole days a week, and only Christmas Day and the afternoon of Good Friday were holidays. And the means for travelling were few, even if one had the time or need. It is true that there was Wortley Station on the single-line track that led to Ouseland, or Harford Station on the main line, but to reach them one had either to walk or pay to be driven in a horse and trap, and that in addition to railway fares. And since the wages of a labourer were twelve shillings a week, and a carpenter or bricklayer was thought well paid at fifteen, travelling by rail was a highly expensive business.

But there were always some of us who had necessary business abroad. Bicycles were rare things in those days, and regarded as new-fangled, and if we had no pony, we walked, even if the journey were one of twelve miles. I remember a man leaving Heathley for a village over twenty miles away, and he came to my father to arrange for the transport of his family and belongings. But he didn't go on that wagon. He rose at dawn and walked to his new home so that it should be partly ready, and such a feat excited no comment. And, of course, we had no desperate need to wander beyond our own confines, since the village was self-supporting. Our gardens, pigsties, heaths, farms, and small shops provided us with all that a simple way of life required.

And yet it could not be said that we were unduly behind the times in the things that mattered. News of national importance reached us at once through the postmistress. There was always the *Eastern Daily Press*, and, on Fridays, its local weekly subsidiary, the *Ouseland and Hareborough Times*. It is true that fashions took some time to reach us, though they were chiefly a concern of the women. And it must be admitted that when the young wits of Heathley called to a parishioner, 'Get your hair cut!' or hollered to some one in haste, 'Whoa, Emma! Mind the paint,' the catchwords were already out of date in the London of their origin.

I was always eager to own a bicycle. For one thing it would have given me greater mobility and enabled me to explore more easily my beloved heaths. The other reason arose when I went to Ouseland to school, for a bicycle would have saved me the long walk to the station, though there I was to forget that a fee which I should be quite unable to afford would be asked for leaving that bicycle in the station yard. But the Homes were living on so precarious a margin that the money for a bicycle was out of all question.

Then a chance arose and I quote it because it must have been the experience of many a village youth. One of the sons of George Dew, the blacksmith who lived by the Mound, was about to acquire a cushion-tyred bicycle and he gave me the offer of his hard-tyred one. Fifteen shillings was the price demanded, and when I had beaten him down to twelve, I ventured to approach my mother. Her solution was that I should work and earn the money. But, as I pointed out, I had worked for my father every harvest of my young life and though promised a yearly trip to Yarmouth, I had never yet seen Yarmouth or a penny of money. To that my mother said she would speak to my father.

Well, I worked that harvest for over five weeks, for my father helped at other harvests besides his own. I also undertook to run the errands of Mrs. Field, wife of the head keeper, and always a good friend to all of us. That brought in a further fourpence a week, and at the end of harvest my father, not too graciously, paid me ten shillings, and the bicycle was mine.

I wish you could see it as I can see it still. Its massive frame weighed probably twice as much as a bicycle of to-day. Its wheels were far too short of their complement of spokes, and they wobbled alarmingly. The front wheel had about an inch of play and there was no difficulty about oiling, for its remaining ball-bearings were visible. The pedals were rickety, too, and there was something peculiar about the handlebars, which could not be adjusted. However tightly one screwed their nut, they would at once slacken. That made steering an adventure, and more than once they came out in my hands, though luckily with no more effect than to deposit me in a ditch or on a grass verge. The chain had a similar obstinacy, for however one adjusted it, it was always coming off.

But I think my method of learning to ride must have been unique. On a Saturday afternoon Tom Edwards and I took that bicycle to Lammas Meadows, where there was a decline that led between our land and the Park to the narrow bridge between the two Watergate Plantations, as they were known. But the advantage of that stretch of road was that there were no ditches at its sides, but only grass verges, and the road itself had rarely any traffic. It is true that at the bottom was the narrow bridge beneath which ran the overflow from a fish-pond, but on that first afternoon its distance of a hundred and fifty yards was to us an object so unattainable as to cease to be a risk.

As owner of the bicycle I mounted first, and then Tom gave me a push. Ten yards on I crashed, straightened the front wheel and the handlebars, and pushed the bicycle back. Tom mounted and was pushed off, and so the process continued.

Soon it was fifty yards before we swerved and fell, and by the end of the afternoon we could almost reach the Watergate bridge. In fact we took turns to ride that bicycle home.

I think I had that bicycle for two years. At intervals I would purloin Brunswick black from my father's paint shop and make it look presentable, but what I remember is the drain it was on my frugal resources, for I had to work a second harvest to settle finally the various bills for repairs. In the end I swopped it for another bicycle, paying in addition the sum of eighteen shillings. But that was an up-to-date modern affair, known to us as a cushion-tyre, even if it wobbled like its predecessor.

The difference between hard tyres and cushion tyres was to us enormous. Whereas the hard tyre made progress a series of bumps on our rough country roads,the slightly hollow cushion tyre had something of the effect of a spring. But it was only when, just before the Boer War, I first tried the pneumatic-tyred bicycle of a friend, that I knew what cycling was. I remember to this day the incredibility of the thing. It wasn't cycling as I had known it; it was floating in space and yet with contact with the ground.

Amazing as it may seem, I rode my own bicycle to Leicestershire. My father, youngest of a very large family, had three sisters living: two in London and the third in a village between Leicester and Lutterworth. On a carrier behind my bicycle I had my necessary belongings in a wicker case, and that morning I was up at three o'clock to begin the journey of some hundred and thirty miles. Somehow I think that same journey was actuated by a faith as great as that of Columbus, and the miracle was that, like Columbus, I arrived. The way I took was by the Fenlands which were flat for riding, but beyond Peterborough I found the unaccustomed hills more than trying. On my return journey I came by Kettering. Higham Ferrers, and St. Neots, and never shall I forget that long eighteen miles of monotony between that last town and The Man Loaded With Mischief at Cambridge.

When I was eighteen I acquired a bicycle that had a free-wheel, and thereby hangs a tale. There was an examination which demanded my presence in London, and about that you will hear later. But that bicycle had been bought on the hire-purchase system and a tremendous faith, and since the family was in one of its financial crises and the railway fares could

2

never have been paid, I naturally accepted the ride as normal and necessary. Into a specially large wicker case went my belongings again, together with all the books I might need for a quick revision, and at dawn I set off for London where I was to stay for the necessary days with my Aunt Lucy.

I had got well past Great Chesterford and had come to a long downhill slope, when suddenly another bicycle drew level with me. Its rider was a country clergyman and he gave me a courteous good-day and began to question me. But the questioning was difficult. We were both free-wheeling, but my bicycle would keep moving ahead and he had to pedal to draw level with me.

'It's extraordinary,' he said at last to me. 'Your bicycle doesn't look so new as mine'—a masterpiece of courteous understatement—'and I must be twice your weight, and yet you keep free-wheeling away from me.'

'I expect it's what I have in my bag, sir,' I said.

'And what *is* in your bag?'

The answer was that among other things there was a complete Liddell and Scott. He stared as if he could not believe me, and as we had by then come to an uphill stretch which made him dismount, I unstrapped the bag and showed him the two mighty tomes. I never saw a man so amused, and with good reason, for I was short and chubby and the books must have rather resembled, and been almost as heavy as, myself. I remember he rode with me almost to Epping, and when we said good-bye he insisted on my accepting a half-crown.

There was another and even greater kindness on that journey, and one which I shall never forget. It was on the homeward trip and I had not left my aunt's house at Wood Green till about four o'clock, for I had such confidence in my powers that I imagined I might complete the hundred miles that summer night. On the journey to town I had had the wind always behind me, but now it was a head wind and it began to freshen. By the time I had reached Great Chesterford I was utterly exhausted, though determined to ride on. Money I had none, for it had all gone on bus fares from Wood Green to South Kensington, and so I was unable to buy a meal.

Great Chesterford was left and then I came to the last of the cottages that straggled by its turnpike. I dismounted and knocked at the door, and a kindly faced woman opened it. I asked for a drink of water and she told me to come in. Then she wormed out of me where I was going, and the fact that I had no food, and in less than no time she had set before me a plate of cold pork, potatoes and greens, with a huge slice of bread. I remember when I left her, stammering my thanks, she only said that if she had a boy she hoped some stranger would do for him the little she had done for me.

On the strength of that meal and in the small hours of the morning, I completed my journey, for after nightfall the wind went down. When I told my father and mother of the kindness of that unknown woman, my father took it as a matter of course, but my mother insisted that the woman should be sent a pair of heath rabbits. As we did not know the name or address, I remember that the label bore the words, 'To the occupier of the last house out of Great Chesterford on the Norwich Road'. Whether or not those rabbits ever reached her I do not know. Many years later I came that way by car and I did my best to find that cottage and that woman. But I found neither. Maybe I had left the little town by some different way, or the little cottage had been destroyed.

And that brings me to the kindliness of Heathley—or should I say rural England?—in my boyhood and youth. For that boyhood I have rarely a nostalgia or regret, for it has irretrievably gone and there is little in it that even day-dreams would wish to alter. Nor is there a nostalgia for the scenes of my youth, even those that also are gone, for I have only to close my eyes to summon and behold them. But where there is always for me a poignancy and a regret is in the remembering of people.

Let me make myself perfectly clear. Heathley was no Arcadia. It had its drunkards and it abounded in what I might call promiscuous love, and of such, according to some ancient poets, was the land of Arcadia. But Heathley had also its hypocrites and petty-minded, its sharpers and fawners, its liars and its petty thieves. I say *petty* because I never remember a burglary in the parish or a theft sufficiently serious to be anything of a wonder, and it is true that most doors in the village were never locked. I remember too, as a small boy, the sensation that was caused when a certain Dick Carter of Stow —a village beyond Brackford—was at large and committing robberies in our countryside. To us children it was as if a

werewolf were abroad, and I remember the relief when Carter
was finally apprehended, and by—of all people—our own
Potter.

But what I do claim is that never have I known a village
so full of kindly people, and I make no differentiation between
Church or Methodists. Among the Methodists one could
discern a kind of communal philanthropy like that that
actuated the Quakers; the feeling, so to speak, that Methodist
blood was thicker than Church water. And there for me,
whether of Church or Chapel, is the poignancy and the regret:
that never by any conceivable chance shall I see those people
again. To see them with the eye of the mind is of no value,
for what I wish is to shake them by the hand, and speak with
them, and thank them for what they were and for the kindnesses bestowed with no thought or possibility of reward or
even an awareness that they were kindnesses at all.

I remember overhearing the conversation of many a village
man in the spring.

'How're you off for plants, George?'

'Not so bad. Might do with a few more savoys, though.'

'Come you along down to mine[1] to-night and you can
have some. I got plenty.'

For those plants a village man would have been ashamed to
charge his neighbour. And it was the same with seed potatoes.
My father, always far too busy with this and that to do the
things that really mattered, would inevitably be short of
seed potatoes in the spring, but at the last moment he
would always remember some neighbour and come back with
a pailful.

I can honestly say that when I was a boy there were in our
village only two people, except two possible witches, whom I
regarded as unkindly or malicious. There was Shaw, husband
of Granny Shaw, who carried tales to my father about my
riding our pony at full gallop through the village, but Shaw
was a consequential, interfering man who never forgot that
he was head coachman to Squire Finch. The other was Squire
Green whom I hated with a fierce intensity, and for reasons
elsewhere related. But take on the other hand old Wyatt, of
whom most of the village youth was in dread. Even his own
men knew the innate kindliness behind the blustering rages.
There were times when I was afraid of him, as when I was

---

[1] My house, similarly *your house* would always be *yours*.

trespassing upon his land, and yet there were times when he went out of his way to do me kindnesses.

I can think of no house in the village of which we had any dread when we were sent to it on errands. At most farm-houses or the houses of those better off than ourselves, there would always be a kindly word and a piece of cake, and to children the poorest cake of others tastes better than the best of one's own. Mrs. Field would always supplement my weekly fourpence with a slice of her cake, and as cake and bread-maker she was always sure of a Flower Show prize. Then there was Mrs. Lake, wife of Dodger Lake, one of our village drunkards. No kinder soul was ever born, and I still remember how, knowing we had no fruit of our own, she would call us into her garden when her plums were ripe and let us help ourselves to windfalls, and often she would shake the tree. There was Josh Till's wife who would give us apples. There was the Goddard family at Brackford, to go into whose house was like going into a second home. There was John Balfour who for months and months gave me out of his scanty leisure private coaching for which he expected no reward, except the success it might bring to myself. Even now it hurts to remember his gratitude when my father would present him with a rabbit, and how he would be wondering perhaps if we were not more in need of it ourselves.

To you those may seem small instances but I could multiply them many times. What I cannot show you is the kindliness on people's faces and the genuine warmth of the spoken word. Perhaps then I may be permitted to put it all in another way, even if you have no great faith in my sincerity.

There is no reason why a single word that I have ever written should last beyond my lifetime, if as long, and yet if it were granted me that out of all those words a something should survive, then I would choose only this. Not that my own name should be remembered, for that is of no importance whatever, but that people should remember those kindly folk of my boyhood; the Methodists who with their Sunday fervour nevertheless lived as if each day were a Sunday; old Wyatt with his passion for the land and his kindly discipline of the men who tilled it; John Pardon of the natural courtesy and deep understanding, who contrived to be both gentleman and villager and retain and bestow respect. Walter Addis, Robert Grinter, John Balfour—the names are too numerous to quote, and all the host of good neighbours whose names in the Heathley of to-day are almost forgotten.

In the Great Winter, when I was eleven years old, disaster befell our potato clamp. I think it was my father who left it open though it was blamed on my brother, but in any case the potatoes were so badly frosted that in less than no time they were all rotten, and since we depended on potatoes for the bulk of our midday and main meal, that was a disaster indeed. But as soon as word got round the village of what had happened, neighbours from everywhere brought us potatoes and my mother has told me that we never felt the loss. But that Great Winter was itself the greatest disaster that came upon Heathley since the days of the Plagues, and many of the debts that were then incurred have never been paid.

The snow lay on the ground for three long months till the March, and the ground was frozen to the consistency of rock. A blizzard began it, and I have reason to remember it well. Half-way to the Vicarage along the Vicarage Road and almost opposite Gaul's Farm was a track known as the Pightle, though how the name should have been transferred from its usual meaning of croft or enclosure to that of a track I do not know. That track ended at a field which we had always farmed, and which backed on the vicarage gardens, and it continued as a public path that emerged at the gravel pit. On that field, known to us as the Pightle Field, my father had built a bullock shed and pigsties, and it was the duty of my brother and myself to feed the stock each morning before breakfast, and that, by the way, was never later than half-past seven.

That early morning, with the blizzard still blowing, we fought our way along the track, and I remember how frightened I was when once I disappeared from view in a drift, with the snow swirling about me and never a sign of my brother. I floundered my way out in a panic and somehow we managed at last to reach the sheds, and I can still feel the agony in my hands as I tried to clean the frozen beet and pulp them, and turn the icy handle of the chaff-cutter. So late were we for breakfast that our father came to look for us, and finally he and a man had to clear a way to the sheds with shovels.

All else that I remember of that winter was the icy cold and that we were on short rations, and, above all, that my father seemed amazingly to be always in the house. For all work in the fields had closed completely down, and, since it was after the loss of Green's work, there was nothing my father could do to bring in money. In the village men were idle for weeks, and since Parish Relief was wholly inadequate, the village was soon in debt to the local shops. How we contrived to live I do not know. Even the rabbits failed us, for poaching was impossible; and when my father tried to snare rabbits on his own land, the ground was so hard that the pegs could not be driven in. It is from then that I remember midday meals of bread and cheese, with my mother instituting the friendly competition of who could eat most bread with least cheese. Another thing I remember was the icy cold; a cold such as the village had never known, and for which its scanty reserves of bedding were inadequate. Our own, like those of many others, were supplemented with stout hessian sacks. And I remember the chilblains from which we all suffered; great cracks in feet and hands and the sudden pain as the healing turpentine was brushed in with a feather. And when the snow finally went and spring came, the Homes, like most of the village, were heavily in debt, and it was a debt that took years to repay.

It was very soon afterwards, just over a year as far as I remember, that we had the Great Wind. It began on a Sunday afternoon, and I can remember sitting in our pew in the little chapel with my mother. Who was preaching I do not know, but before the service began there was no noticeable wind, and yet before it ended the windows were rattling with threats of broken glass, and so loud was the roar that the voice of the preacher was often drowned. I remember, too, that the evening preacher should have come from a fairly distant village and that he never arrived. And there was no wonder, for every road for miles around was blocked by fallen trees, and it was days before some of them were cleared.

Heathley, particularly towards the east, was largely woods, though by that I do not mean that there were more woods than arable land or pasture. What I do mean is that you were never out of the sight of woods, and the farther from the main roads and tracks, the more woods there were. How many trees crashed in those woods on that Sunday cannot be computed. Oaks and pines lay scattered everywhere as if the devil himself had run amok. But that is not the point. From then on I knew those woods as well as any keeper. I loved short cuts and hated beaten tracks and there was not a Heathley wood that I did not intimately know, and therefore my evidence is enough when I say that of all those trees not one in a thousand was ever removed. Where they fell, they lay and rotted, and the remains of some are there till this day. For that storm made a natural undergrowth in woods that had always been thin beneath the trees. There the pheasants could nest and thrive, and a village man would have risked both house and living if he had ventured there in search of fuel. And without any further harping on the Game Laws I will only add that the rabbits multiplied there too, and since a tenant farmer had no right of entry to the woods that lodged the rabbits that devoured his corn, it would not be wholly unreasonable to call that Great Wind as devastating in its effects as had been the Great Winter that preceded it.

After the coming of Green the social strata of Heathley were not so easily defined. Before his coming the village was the village, and Hall and Vicarage were Hall and Vicarage, and that was that. We did not bless the squire and parson and their relations or pray to be kept in our proper stations, for those stations were centuries old and we were not even aware of them. Radicals like my father and William Cash might rail against squires and parsons in general, and Game Laws and endowments, and despair at the subservience and disunity of the labouring man, and yet tacitly accept the system and their own part in it. But the private life of Hall and Vicarage was as far removed from our own as that of Her Majesty, and Finch, though a just man and a fair landlord, was never lavish of his presence, so that his public appearances lent a kind of awe to his state. John Pardon was different, though he could unbend with no cheapening of himself or his office. But when we passed the Vicarage and saw tennis-parties in progress on the courts, with the white blouses of the ladies and the blazers of the men, or when we saw the traps or dog-carts and their smart coachmen arriving for some call or garden-party, we even felt in some vague way that the village was being honoured by such things. Tennis and golf were games that conveyed nothing to us, and I doubt if one of us had the faintest idea how they were played.

But with the arrival of Green there arose a curious and detestable middle stratum. Previously the rest of us had been a community of equals. A farmer might possess more pounds than we had ha'pence, but we met and greeted each other as equals, and equals we were. Then came flunkeydom and snobbery. As I have said elsewhere, a new hierarchy arose, of butler, housekeeper and those in the village whom they deemed suitable company, and on their heels the footmen and keepers with their own subsidiary cliques. Then at shooting-parties were the visiting valets and personal staff and ladies' maids. In their patronage of the village the Lion became the head-quarters of the men, and soon the village would be quoting their opinions and their London witticisms. And while the village had never lacked its toadies or those with an eye to the main chance, now their number increased with the opportunities for advancement under Green's patronage. I do not say that Green was aware of such things. I am almost sure that he was ignorant of the discrimination of his housekeeper —his first housekeeper, a tall, domineering woman—against the Methodist children in the presentation of Christmas gifts, but what I am sure of is that before Green had been in the village a couple of years, the whole character of the place had undergone a subtle change.

But for the Homes, the village was always divided into two parts—our immediate surroundings being the principal one. I still remember that so rarely did I go down the Shopleigh Road that my visits there were a kind of furtiveness in which was a certain fear. What fear I do not know, and doubtless it passed as I grew older, but I know that I hated on wet days to pass the Crown for then one could see the labourers, and two or three notorious drunkards among them, sitting at their beer. My father neither drank nor smoked, and so well had the fate and ever-present example of our village drunkards been dinned into our ears, that those drinkers of beer seemed to a small boy as dreadful as the demons enjoying themselves in the very mouth of hell.

We children then were scrupulously kept to our own end of the village, except when sent on errands, and often then the centre of the village could be avoided. When we went to Mrs. Field's, for instance, we were told to go by Stile Meadow, which ran from opposite the vicarage past Josh Till's to the Wortley Road. Later, when we had the great barn that stood opposite the Eagle and the school, with the stables and sties behind it, I would often have to work there, and as that barn was the village parliament house, there was much that I saw and heard that would never otherwise have reached my eyes and ears.

But in case you should be thinking me something of a prig in the matter of beer drinking, let me say that when I was still a boy I was present one harvest evening at a field where the last of the corn was being cut. I think a larger field was being finished elsewhere at the same time, for I remember that I was almost the only boy who was chasing the rabbits. When it was all over and the rabbits had been divided among us, the farmer poured out the last of the beer. Perhaps the sight of my perspiring face made him hand me a mug, and I remember I took it with no qualms of conscience. But before I could take a first swig, the smell of that beer was so repulsive that I smiled sheepishly and handed the mug back.

When I was still short of eighteen I was sent one evening with a written message to a certain Colonel. I was shown into a kind of lounge where a huge potted palm stood in one corner, and when the Colonel came in and read the note, he asked me if I would take a drink. He added that he was having one himself, and then asked what I would have. I tactfully said that I would have whatever he was having. Even in those days I was nothing if not adventurous.

The butler came in with a tray and served the Colonel first. 'Not too much soda,' the Colonel told him, and then he came to me. The whisky was poured.

'How much soda?' he asked me.

'Not too much,' I said in imitation of the Colonel, and I can't help thinking to-day that his eyebrows must have raised.

The Colonel took a swig at his drink and I took one at mine. I had read in books about whiskies and sodas and was anticipating some sort of thrill, the sort that always came before sipping a glass of my mother's home-made ginger wine. But the taste of that liquid was indescribable. It was something like methylated spirits and altogether so nauseating that as I gulped it down I was wondering at once if I were going to be sick. But fortunately for me the Colonel was at his desk writing an answer to the note, and the contents of my glass were surreptitiously emptied round the base of the palm. When the Colonel had written the answering note and was ready for me, I was hypocrite enough to pretend to have just finished my glass.

So much for my first appearance in society with a butler to pour me a drink. As for the developments in my taste, all I will say is that oddly enough the only way I can drink whisky is with soda. And of the good few I have since consumed I will say this, that never did I have one without recalling the first I ever took, and sometimes I would wonder what curious effect if any, it had on the Colonel's potted palm.

Chapter III

THE VILLAGE—*continued*

TO the readers of William Cobbett, and I hope there are many, the history of the farm labourer in Norfolk will come as no shock. If I concern myself solely with the labourer in Breckland it is because Norfolk is a large county and the conditions of the labourer varied from area to area. Great and progressive landlords like Coke were as fathers to their immense families —and one can so regard their villages—and even Cobbett admits that nowhere did he hear anything but the highest praise of men like Coke.

But the soil of Breckland was poor, and the district itself remote from progress, and in the great depressions the lot of the farm labourer was incredibly hard. In the Hungry Forties malnutrition was rife and hundreds of young Norfolk men who had managed somehow to scrape together the passage money, emigrated to Canada and the States. Education for a labourer's family was almost non-existent. The grip of distress was so cruel that at the earliest age children were at work and supplementing the meagre wage. The Homes, for instance, were once important holders of land in Heathley, and then in my grandfather's time the final disaster came, for he died as the result of a fall from a stack, and my grandmother was left with a family of ten children, the eldest of whom was fifteen. The land had to be given up and all the children had to work. My father was working at the age of seven for a farmer at a wage of a shilling a week, and his schooling was the result of his own efforts and in his scanty leisure. In my sophisticated youth I rather despised my father's handwriting, which was large and clumsy. I hope, shamedly enough at this moment, that he was never aware of my thoughts. But many or most had neither the leisure nor the inward urge to seek an education of their own. The years had cowed them too much, and fifty years ago in Heathley there were still many who could neither read nor write.

The very word *labourer* was a kind of reproach. It meant the lowest form of work and the worst paid. It was, in a way, the lowest unit by which all else was calculated. And if the labourer tried to supplement his starvation wage by poaching, then there were the Game Laws—their spring guns and man-traps, and their threats of transportation. His condition was one of subservience. His life's sentence was to work for six or seven days each week for the duration of his years, and at the end of that long vista was the workhouse. No wonder that in my boyhood the labourer was both colourless and politically inarticulate. When he ventured to speak it was guardedly. At elections he hollered with and for his masters, but the sign of abundant hope was that he voted for those whom he secretly deemed his friends. Had the ballot not been secret, the change in status of the labourer might have been deferred another fifty years.

But the more dry-as-dust history, and economics and political speculation are not the province of this book. What you may like to know—and it is a thing that has often puzzled myself—is how the labourer of my boyhood managed to live on his twelve shillings a week, though to many it was a great sum compared with his grandfather's seven. So I obtained from my mother—now in her eighty-third year—a kind of budget. But before I submit it, there are other things which must be made clear.

Rent, clothes, and replacements of household gear are not included. They were paid for by a man's taking-work:[1] the four pounds or so that he might earn extra at harvest, and other monies for chopping out[2] beet, or at haysel. And the budget is not for a labourer with a large family, since some of that family would be at work and their wages would supple-ment his own. The budget is for a man with a wife and four to five young children, and is roughly what my mother would

---

[1] Piece-work.   [2] Singling.

have spent herself. And since our standard of living was rather higher than that of a labourer's family, there are things that may be deleted.

Pork, for instance, which might have come from the labourer's own pig. Such a pig would be acquired when young from his employer and would be paid for when it was killed, as would the barley-meal purchased for its final fattening and the supers on which it was first fed. Some of that pork would be retained to go into the salt pot. Some would go to a man who had provided pork from his own pig, and so by that system of deferred payments and homely barter, a labourer might have little pork on which hard cash was spent. Vegetables cost work only, and the small sum needed for seeds. And rabbits cost little or nothing according to how they were come by.

But there is something else to consider. The village drunkard was happily either an unmarried man or a man whose family had largely grown up, and I admit frankly that what happened to the family of such other heavy drinkers as I remember, I cannot say. But take a man who had a drink now and then; say a half-pint a day, and his ounce or two ounces of shag a week. That came to at least a shilling, and he had in addition his club money and his insurance, and those might be put as ninepence. Add threepence for eventualities, and the amount received by his wife could not have exceeded ten shillings.

Here, then, are the items.

	s.	d.
14 large loaves @ 2¼d	2	6
4 lb. pork	2	0
1 lb. butter	0	9
1½ lb. pork-cheese[1]	0	6
1½ lb. pig's-fry	0	6
1 can of skimmed milk per day @ 1d.	0	7
½ stone flour	0	9
4 lb. sugar	0	8
½ lb. tea (Bonus tea prices are given as women would buy it on account of the gifts presented for its coupons)	0	10½
¼ lb. cocoa	0	4
1 lb. cheese	0	6
½ lb. each of currants and raisins	0	4

[1] Brawn.

1 lb. bacon	0	7
Lard and dripping	0	6
Eggs (1d. when scarce and ½d. when plentiful	0	?
Oddments, as matches, soap, starch, paraffin	0	6
½ cwt. coal	0	7½
Bloaters at ½d. each		?

Total 12 6

Prices of different things doubtless varied all over England, but those are the Breckland prices, and checked with the price lists of a village grocer who was in business fifty years ago. And the first thing you will say is that they make no sense. Things like jam (3 lb. for 11d.) treacle (2 lb. for 6d.) and the luxury of a tin of salmon (6½d.) have been omitted and may be set off against a saving in meat, and even then you can scarcely reduce that total to the sum of ten shillings. The answer apparently is that families ran into debt. That is true when times were hard, as in the Great Winter, but generally it was certainly not true. Where, then, is the catch or the fallacy?

The answer lies, I think, in what I might call the imponderables. In *Autumn Fields* I mentioned Long Harry and his monstrous pitching-fork. Imagine my delight when I received a letter from his son, Fred, who had read that book. It was Fred's older brothers and sisters whom I knew well and I recall him only faintly, but this is what he told me. His father's pitching-fork he remembered well. That father had been a kind one to his family though a heavy drinker, and, said Fred, 'The wonder to me still is how we managed to live and be clean and tidy and respectable. We couldn't have done it but for my mother, who darned and mended till all hours of the night and took no thought of herself.'

That is what I mean by the imponderables. Where a woman goes short for the sake of her children, the spending is less and the budget can somehow be balanced. I know that the sacrifices of my own mother can never be repaid. Of Fred's mother I knew little, though now I wish I had known her better. But all over Heathley, there must have been similar women who saved and schemed and went short, and regarded it not even as a duty.

Heathley families were generally large, and I remember
many where an annual baby was a normal event till the total
had reached ten or twelve. 'Kittle' Webster, who lived in one
of the remaining cottages at Little Heathley and was later
cowman for Wyatt, was the father of such a family, and I
remember my father, who often had business with Wyatt,
laughing at 'Kittle' when a family addition arrived.

'No more for me,' 'Kittle' used to say with a sideways
shake of the head. 'After this I'm hangin' up the old harness
in the shed.'

But in spite of the vow backed by that homely metaphor,
babies continued to arrive. As for 'Kittle' himself, a lantern-
jawed but genial man, I have often wondered about his nickname, or if by some strange persistence it was no nickname at
all, for Kettle was a common enough first name among our
Scandinavian ancestors. But most lads and men in Heathley
had nicknames, and their origins were obscure. Elsewhere I
mentioned Bertie's—Alley Dew. I remember among others a
young Carman whose nickname was Jam, because at a church
treat he had announced that he was fond of it. There was a
Large, whose nickname was the blasphemous one of Jeedo,
for when as a child he sang in the Sunday school the refrain
of a Moody-Sankey hymn, some impediment in his speech
made the words, 'Yes, Jeedo loves me.' Porky, the nickname
of an old roadman, seems obvious, but what is the origin of
Dooter, given to another of the Larges? Nor could you ever
guess the origin of the nickname Gramp, given to another
boy, for it was this. His grandfather was digging one spring
day and the boy joined him.

'May I dig here, Grampa?' he asked.

'Whuh, no!' the old man told him, horrified. 'That's my
onion bed!'

What I wonder is if you see anything else in those nicknames: how self-contained the village was, for instance, so that
the smallest happening to the most insignificant of its inhabi-
tants was of such importance as to be a matter for talk and
laughter and to leave a nickname in its trail.

As to the labourer, it is symptomatic of his history and
status in Breckland that Heathley had no crafts beyond those
connected with the cultivation of the land. Blacksmiths,
wheelwrights, and carpenters supplied the needs of farmers and
villagers and no more, but at Wortley, just beyond the railway

station, was the forge of the Edwards brothers, whom I knew well, for they were for long years members of the Wortley cricket side. But they were craftsmen in metal as well as shoers of horses and repairers of agricultural implements, and I remember as a boy seeing a pair of gates which they made for —I believe—Didlington Hall, with a strength and virility of main design but the ornament as delicate as filigree.

Even our thatchers could not work with reed, though reeds abounded in the fens of Cranberry and the margins of the meres. It was true that many could make clay lump, but that is a simple process, but the building of flint houses, or houses with brick framework panelled with hewn flint, was never carried out in my time. When the dry flint wall of the church-yard collapsed, there was much wagging of beards as to the method of repairing it, and there was much wasted labour before the right method was arrived at. Then there was the split pale fencing which was much used for the boundaries of parks. When Colonel Pewtrance of Brackford required split oak for his estate boundaries, there was no man in the district who knew the craft or had the tools, and a man was finally imported from as far away as Yarmouth.

But if there was much that the labourer had forgotten, there was much that he had remembered. I recall veterinary practices that must have survived from almost the dark ages, and a farmer once lent me a book, in the faded handwriting of his father, that had cures and charms and recipes that smacked of witchcraft and heaven knows what antiquity. I wish I could remember some of those cures, with their dried and powdered toads and herbs collected at special times of the moon. There were men, too, who claimed to have a recipe for a magic sort of bottle. If the cork was taken out in a field, so strong and potent was the scent that a horse would follow the owner. I often wished I had owned such a bottle, for Grey Jack was a pony of devilish cunning and often I took so long in catching him that I lost most of my breakfast.

Superstition lingered long in Breckland. Men were weather-wise as their fathers had been and consulted the same omens. I have mentioned the belief that stones grew, a belief which is met with to this day. Many years ago I came across a pamphlet giving the results of certain experiments that dis-proved the influence of the moon on plant growth, so I made my gardener read it.

'That just go to show you,' he said when he gave me the pamphlet back, and then after a few days had gone there came this.

'Better be gettin' them so-and-so seeds in, sir, if we don't want to miss the moon.'

It was always, and still is, the same with the influence of the moon on the weather: a belief which is the peculiar property of the unscientific rural mind, or perhaps I should say the mind that remembers only the favourable changes of weather that have coincided with changes of the moon and conveniently forgets the rest. And so with those hazy notions of cause and effect that prophesy wet summers from observation of oak and ash and hard winters from an abundance of berries.

One thing may be puzzling you about Heathley—that if families were large, then there must have been a surplus population. It is a question to which I have devoted much time and research and I can still arrive at no answer. What seems true is this, that even before the arrival of Green there was little surplus labour. With his coming the surplus was absorbed, as was any slight increase. But girls always left the village for domestic service elsewhere, and it was just at the opening of the new century that the pneumatic tyre became common and bicycles cheaper and more easily acquired. That was when the migrations to the towns really began though there had always been a certain trend. It was, for instance, the ambition of most village youths to join a police force, and those who attained the right stature did so. When they were established in their new homes they would find openings for younger brothers, and so the denudation began. But with the larger exodus of the new century the process was necessarily accelerated, and the more who left, the more who followed.

The Services were not popular; indeed the Army was looked on as a refuge for rascals generally and those who fled to avoid the cost of promiscuous paternity. I remember only one man who became a soldier, and the story has its amusing side.

Many young man of Heathley joined the Volunteers, but at the outbreak of the South African War when men were called for, one only volunteered to go, and he was Dooter Large. The village therefore regarded Dooter as a kind of hero, and just before his much delayed departure there was a collection in the village to speed him on his patriotic way. I do not know to how much it amounted, but I imagine it was a fair sum. But Dooter, as it so happened, was never called upon to leave the country, and all that remains as a memorial is a son who was born to him later, and who received the Christian names of Kitchener Kimberley!

One young man did go for a soldier, as we called it, and that was Fred Lake, son of Dodger, and he became a marine. Years afterwards, by a strange coincidence, he became a gardener of mine, and in gardens into which had been incorporated the garden he had known as a boy with its trees from which his mother had so often given us her windfall plums.

One of the scorns in which soldiers were held by the too-godly was the matter of heavy drinking, and Fred was no exception to prove the rule an arbitrary one. Never have I known a more lovable character, more trustworthy or more loyal. Joan, the only one of my nieces to be born in my house, loved him as the best of uncles. Fred had twice been a sergeant of marines, and had twice been broken for over-staying leave, and in my service there would come times when the call was too strong. Then he would disappear for a week perhaps, and when the drinking bout ended with his money, he would return. In his eyes would be something of shame and an expectation of reprimand, and I think he was hurt even more because such reprimands never came.

It was amusing and chastening how he would impute to me a vast and intimate knowledge of the world. We would be working side by side in the garden, and yarning, maybe, and suddenly he would say, 'Something like that happened to me when I was in Madagascar. When was you in Madagascar, sir?' Or it might be Peru or Patagonia. But the feat of which he was most proud was when as a sergeant of marines he held an inquest on a Chinese woman up the Yangtse. What he never mentioned was that he had been twice decorated for valour and mentioned at least twice more in dispatches. When a few years ago I heard that he had gone, I spent a restless day. If there is gardening in Elysium I would like to spend part of my days there with Fred.

As to the leisure of the labourer, the hard truth is that once his children had begun to arrive, his leisure ceased. Hours were from six to six from Valentine's to Michaelmas, and the summer nights meant work on gardens or allotments, with a last half-hour maybe at a pub. In the summer, bedtime was never later than ten, and in the winter most families were asleep soon after nine.

One night a week he would attend at the village lodge of his Friendly Society to pay his dues and take part in its business or its simple functions. On Whit-Sundays he never missed the church parade of his Society and on Flower Show Day there would be a holiday. On Sundays he might take a walk in those best clothes that his father perhaps had worn, and in his later years would attend church or chapel. If there were a parish meeting he would often be there, but always inarticulate and fearful of taking sides.

In his younger days too, if somehow he had managed to acquire a bicycle, he would often go fishing. Our ponds and meres abounded in coarse fish, and thundery weather was held to be the best, and the huge bream and tench that were caught made useful additions to the family larder, as did eels, though they were most often caught with spears. For my own part I never caught a fish as large as a herring, even though one summer I was smitten with the fever and spent almost every night away at the Top Breck. For rod I had a long willow pole, and the hook and float were bought at Cash's shop. Bait was invariably worms, and when I had cast the line neatly between the clumps of weed I would read one of those novels of Scott that John Balfour lent me, with now and again an eye on the unmoving float. Maybe there were few fish in that Top Breck pit, but farther afield I was never allowed to go.

A subsequent brother-in-law of mine was more fortunate when fishing in the meres, and many is the fish I have eaten that fell to his home-made rod. Which brings me to one of the most flagrant digressions, and I would not tell it were it not as unusual a dream as I have ever heard.

This brother-in-law, now dead, was also interested in antiques, with a particular liking for grandfather clocks. One night after he had been fishing he dreamt that he was walking by the side of a mere when he heard a squeaky voice calling for help. After some time he located the sound, which came from under the water against his feet, so he groped with his hands among the weeds and what came away was a tiny man.

This man expressed his gratitude for having been released from the weeds.

'As a reward,' he said, 'I'll show you the finest grandfather clock you ever saw in your life.'

I gather he was no bigger than a finger but the cottage to which he led the way was high enough in the ceiling for my brother-in-law to stand upright. But when he had a good look round that first room there was never a sign of a clock.

'Where's the clock you were going to show me?' he asked the little man.

'This *is* the clock,' he was told.

And so it was. That house was a clock. The room in which they were standing was the bottom pedestal, up the stairs were the swinging pendulum and even the weights, and the attic was the hood containing the works! The pity of it was that he so roared with laughter at the disclosure that he woke himself and my sister, not that the story hadn't a satisfactory enough ending.

This mention of fish reminds me of a story that I heard my father relate a score of times. In his boyhood there was in the village a man who was something of a simpleton and very much of a thief. But because of his artless mind his various thefts were glossed over, though those who employed him generally kept a careful watch.

Now at the West Farm there was a large and ancient carp in a tank, and this man, whom we will call Tom, was working in the gardens there. Then, in the course of the afternoon the famous carp was missing. It was useless to charge Tom with the theft for one could never have got sense out of him. And he had not been home for dinner for his boy had brought that midday meal. A surreptitious search of Tom's frail[1] basket revealed no carp, and the farmer was at his wit's end what to do. But the Superintendent at Harford was a relation and Tom was not due to knock off till six, so the farmer drove to Harford and acquainted the police with the facts.

That evening when Tom was going home along Vicarage Road, a smart trap met him. The police superintendent handed the reins to his man and jumped out.

'Tom, you're just the very man I want to see,' he said. 'I've got just the job that'll suit you down to the ground.'

'And what's that, sir?' asked Tom.

'A postilion's job at Ouseland,' he was told. 'The only

---

[1] Rush or wicker.

trouble is whether the livery will fit you. Perhaps I'd better
have a see.'

He set the frail basket aside after making sure no carp was
in it and then began feeling Tom all over.

'Yes, shoulders seem all right, so do the waist. Now what
about the legs?'

'That's all right, sir,' Tom suddenly told him, with a
mixture of craft and innocence. 'You needn't do no more
searchin'. I sent that carp home by the boy.'

A history of the tenant farmers as I knew them would take
a chapter in itself. The first with whom I was acquainted was
the father of William Cash, who was known as Tailor Cash,
and he then had the farm later taken over by Ben Gaul.

I suppose I was no more than eight years old and I had
come into the possession of a tennis ball. Tailor Cash came
down the Vicarage Road and was proceeding slowly towards
the Mound when I threw that ball, and with no malice afore-
thought. I think, indeed, that I was throwing it and then
picking it up and throwing it again, but that particular throw
happened to hit Cash clean in the middle of his high-crowned
hat. I remember his shaking his stick at me and my running
home terrified at what I had done.

Old Cash had the reputation of a miser, though if it was
merited I cannot say. I do remember his clothes which were
black, long faded to a bottle green, and that, like old Wyatt,
he wore garments long out of fashion even with us—the coat
reaching to the knees with immense pockets and buttons, and
tight trousers with cloth leggings. It was said of him that he
fed his horses on the minimum diet and I distinctly remember
the village joke about him, that when the ribs of his horses
showed too clear he would tell man or boy to let them have a
good blow-out in the horse-pond.

The greatest of all our farms was West Farm. Its house was
a pleasant Georgian building overlooking a meadow that had
the air of once having been a park, and it had ornamental
gardens which even in my time were reasonably well kept.
But its farm buildings were immense. Its mill had ceased to
exist, as had its blacksmith's shop, but the name of the latter
persisted in the name of the field by the Six-pits, a field which
I have good cause to remember, for years afterwards it was
to cost me a considerable sum of money in the depression

between the wars. I do not know how many men and boys worked there fifty years ago, but I should put the number as no more than ten at the most. My father used to tell me that in his father's time there were no less than seventy who worked there—a little township in itself. The mill alone served all the district, and from the still immense range of buildings, one can be certain that the seventy of my grandfather's time was no exaggeration.

When I first knew it it was in the occupation of an elderly farmer named Breeze, whose housekeeper was a close friend of my mother. Then all its fields as far as Cranberry were in full cultivation and I remember the line of cornstacks on land which I was to live to see invaded by bracken and overrun by rabbits. The Plains were part of its pasture and I remember the flock of twenty score ewes which roamed that rough pasture in summer, and the strawed hurdles on the home swede fields when the ewes were there for early spring lambing

The Crawfords along the Shopleigh Road were father and son, and the son had a large family whom I knew well, for they were Methodists. All I will say of the son is that he was much of a mystery to me as a boy, for he suffered from some mental complaint or kink, and though well enough in health, would spend months in bed. The main farm work fell then on Grandfather Crawford, as we knew him. He was a lean, bowed, active man, who walked at a tremendous pace and seemed possessed of an inexhaustible vitality. I remember, too, his little twinkling eyes, and his sparrow-like alertness, and above all, his prayer-meeting prayers and his quick, 'Amy! Amy!' which were his amens when some point that a preacher made rejoiced his fervent heart.

Boddy, whose farm-house and buildings were in the centre of the village, was another ancient survival, and a man of furious tempers and blasphemies like old Wyatt. It was he who at hawkies would sing the two songs of which I remember only the titles—*I've lost my spotted cow* and *Yonder shine the moon*. But his voice was such a scrannel pipe that men had hard work to keep a straight face, and that would bring about a scene that I more than once witnessed, though I must admit that I never had the courage to be provocative myself.

It would be when Boddy was having a pig killed in his yard that lay open, except for a gate, to the main road near Cash's shop. Somehow pigs seemed usually to be killed in the late

afternoon, so that before the operation was over, the boys—
and the louts among them principally—would be at the gate
and watching the proceedings, and with the expectation of
obtaining the bladder. Finally one would be deputed to ask
for the bladder, and then when he had secured it, there would
begin a quavering chorus in imitation of Boddy's voice:

'I've lost my spotted cow.'

In a flash the old man would be transformed. He would
snatch up a stick or any handy weapon and with a furious,
'Bla-a-st ye!' would make for the gate. The innocent who had
not scattered would suffer for the guilty for he would lay
about him on the buttocks of any who were handy, and all the
time would be roaring in rage. In a minute the whole area
would be cleared and all that would be seen of those urchins
would be specks still running to a farthest safety

I know only two kinds of farmers, and the ones who have
my chief respect are those who work on their land: working
farmers as one might call them. Boddy was such, but the one
who succeeded him was of the other kind. His name was
Shepherd, distinctive because he had a wooden leg, and
notorious because as a school attendance officer he had been
very much of a bully. It was his son who was nominally in
charge of the farm, but the son would be at markets, and never
miss a Hareborough agricultural show, and when he drove
abroad it was wearing a straw hat and in a rubber-tyred gig.
That farm was poor land and had broken many hearts, and its
new tenants, who became objects of secret derision, remained
on it only a year or two.

Of the Kerridge farming I remember only one thing—my
father always sneering at his method of growing swedes and
beet. For Kerridge was a believer in covering the ground. His
rows were closer than normal and the crop thinned only
sparingly, and I remember once my father taking me to see
the crop of another farmer and trying to prove to me the
fallacy in Kerridge's reasoning that quantity meant quality
and weight. But what you yourself—whether countryman or
townsman—might like to see is a balance-sheet of one of our
Heathley farms of almost fifty years ago. It is an authentic
document and the farmer as good a one as was ever in the
parish, though his farm was fairly small. The only alterations
I have made are of spelling and arrangement. It is ten years

since I took it out, and the handwriting has only slightly faded. It is clear and easily decipherable, and has something of the sturdiness of the man who wrote it.

C.	£	s.	d.	D.	£	s.	d.
OATS. 72 coomb @ 8s.	28	16	0	Seed corn, small seeds, cake meal and oats	33	9	0
BARLEY. 133 coomb @ 12/6	83	2	6	Wages	82	8	0
WHEAT. 104 coomb @ 13/6	70	4	0	Rent and rates. Tithe	116	0	0
Five fat bullocks	94	0	0	Cow	18	0	0
Pigs	23	0	0	Household	31	0	0
Butter, eggs, fowls, etc.	85	0	0	Smith, vet. and wheelwright	6	5	0
Various	4	7	6	Sundries	17	2	0
				3 young bullocks	22	10	0
Total	£388	10	0	Total	£326	14	0

Profit £61 16 0

A farm therefore *could* be run at a profit. But, whoever you are, countryman or townsman, look carefully at those accounts again to see if you notice the remarkable or indicative about them. I do not mean that you are to hunt for errors. I take that account to be correct in its essentials, for I knew the man who drew it up.

Somehow I do not think you'll have spotted what it is that is so important. It is this. Look at butter and eggs. Those were solely the results of the work of the farmer's wife, and often, in addition, she had to lend a hand with milking the small herd and feeding the stock. But that farmer also had a young son of working age, and there is nothing put down for his wages, for he received little or none. As for that farmer, he rose at dawn in the summer and long before it in winter, and his working day would last till almost the moment when he went to bed. He worked far longer hours than any of his men and he worked as hard or harder. *For that work, and for that of his wife and son, he was richer at the end of a year by sixty-one pounds.* And the year quoted was a good year. What was such a man to do when the year was bad or he suffered loss of stock or there came a time of depression?

If I stand up and proclaim that I am a first-class swimmer —than which nothing is farther from the truth—I am perfectly safe so long as I never allow myself to be seen in the water. In the same way it would be folly for a bad farmer to claim to be an expert when his fields were open to the inspection of his neighbours. I would add, too, that however conservative or die-hard a man may be, he will rarely be such to the gross detriment of his pocket. A farmer may have his own views but only a fool would fail to profit by the example and plain experience of his neighbours, provided the farming is done on much the same soil.

It was Wyatt who set at Hill Farm the standard for the village. You may not be a farmer but you will easily understand the underlying principles, for if you are anything of a gardener you will know at least that there are crops which ought not to follow year after year upon the same ground. The sequence of farming crops was—to make a beginning— wheat. That was followed by beet or swedes which allowed cleaning of the ground, and if the swedes were folded by sheep, the land was automatically trodden and dunged. In the third year that land grew barley or oats, but it was usual to sow a ley—layer as we called it—of grass and clover when the barley was established, and the two crops grew together, with the barley far overtopping the layer. When the barley was cut, the close crop of layer grew on and in the fourth year became a crop of hard hay. In that fourth autumn its second crop would be folded perhaps with sheep; then it might be dunged as well and was ploughed for winter wheat. That was the four-crop rotation.

Let us look deeper though still simply. Take the bullock as the corner-stone of the theory, and assume, too, that the cost of his fattening will be less than the price he fetches at market; that, in other words, it pays to fatten stock. Now bullocks were fed on chaff and chopped beet and swedes, except for cake to give the final fattening, and those things the land grew. But the land could grow nothing without manure, and it was the bullocks who provided that manure from the straw bedding which the land grew. The more bullocks, the more muck, and the more muck, the better the crops. *But*, and here is the other side of the picture as affecting poor land, if bullocks no longer pay; if, say, it is political or economic policy to import meat more cheaply than a farmer can produce it, then the whole system falls to the ground. No bullocks, no muck, no crops. 'As simple as that?' you say incredibly, and for our light lands I say emphatically yes. And I will not labour the point. All I would ask is that you should take such things into account when considering the ultimate ruin of an English village.

Those simple principles were those followed by Wyatt, and therefore by the rest of the village, and Wyatt had no more enthusiastic follower than my father. That is not to say that old-fashioned methods did not still persist. A man would not be a man but a machine if he too slavishly followed a model, and all our farmers had their peculiarities and preferences. And those who were prepared to slave managed to get a living. Some, whose crops were hard hit by the depredations of Green's pheasants or the rabbits from his woods, would go to him, cap in hand, and I will do him this justice to say that I seem to remember many who at times received compensation. But after that despicable political business that cost him Green's work, my father was too proud to make such an approach, and our hungry land was back-breakingly farmed and rarely showed a profit.

When Wyatt left he was succeeded by agents. I scarcely expect belief when I state that I heard one such say that it was not an economic proposition to cart muck to the land, and that thereafter began the main use of artificials. One such agent had in his office—that office at the wood-yard where Squire Finch himself once used to meet his tenants each Michaelmas Day—a huge map of the holdings under him with each field marked. According to him the secret of farming was to take an account of each such separate field and know the cost of its labour and artificials and to set those off against returns. Fields not showing a profit should be discarded for arable and put down to grass. All I will say is that one thing rejoices my heart. I lived to see the last of the agents scuttled, as it were, from the village, with their charts and graphs and the flicking of forelocks that accompanied their village progress. But the harm had been done, and the land was starved and ruined beyond repair. 'But bullocks might still have saved it?' you may say. Maybe they would, but the time had come when to fatten stock was to face a certain loss. But such recollections bring, as you will have discerned, both bitterness and anger. It is hard to write of them dispassionately. Let us get back then to the village of forty-five years ago.

I have often met in autobiographies accounts of the hearing of the news of the death of Queen Victoria, and because the impact on the minds of my contemporaries was a tremendous one. I can see, as if it were this very night, an early evening in our house. The lamp had been long lit and the green cloth put on the table. My sisters were playing Ludo and I was reading a book by the fire. My mother was darning or mending and her foot gently rocked the cradle in which the baby was sleeping, and my father in his big chair by the window was reading the *Ouseland and Hareborough Times*. Then suddenly there came a tap at the front door. That was a strange thing, for practically every caller, except the Reverend and Mrs. Pardon, used the back, and at any time of the night.

'Whuh, who can that be, mother?' my father asked.

I was already at the door and opening it.

'Mr. Downs, mother,' I said.

'Come in, Jimmy!' hollered my father, for the caller was old Jimmy—'Monkey'—Downs of Brackford.

'No, I won't come in,' Jimmy said, and his voice had an unusual solemnity. 'I thowt I'd just let you know, together, that I was at the post office and they just told me the Queen is dead.'

That was all, but I remember the hush that fell on our little room. A personal bereavement was as nothing to it. It was as if the world for a moment stood still. Or that we were suddenly among things strange and unknown, and wanderers without chart or compass.

If I were asked to give my impressions of the coming of the Edwardian age and its impacts, and if, therefore, I cast about in my mind to make a reply, I should see only the queerest flashes of memory to illuminate the most trivial of things. But those are the sort of tricks my memory often plays me. When for instance, I think of the Vicarage, I never do so without recalling the first time I saw it over fifty years ago. I do not remember being impressed by the drive, or the house, or by the maids in their pink dresses or by a sight of the Reverend himself. All I see is an attic above one of the stables. On the floor is hay and on the hay are thousands of apples. But they are no longer apples but the pulp and chewings that the rats have left, for my father had been called in to devise a means to destroy the rats and he had taken me with him.

When now I think of the coming of the Edwardian era, and my mind is somewhat blurred by latter-day assessments of its graciousness and stateliness, I think of one thing. It is a Flower Show day and there are guests at the Hall. Mrs. Green —I think she was French, and I know she was very much younger than Green himself—has honoured the sports by her presence and she and her guests are in their private enclosure. I, for some reason happen to pass it, and so near that I can almost touch the great lady herself. I hear the little trill in her laugh and the mysterious loveliness of her voice. Above all I notice the dress she is wearing, and I can see it to this very day. It is a pale maroon in colour and even to my boyish eyes it has a grandeur—yet not a grandeur but more of a uniqueness— that gives me a mysterious thrill. The bodice is tight and the neck high, and there is about it something of the look of those uniforms of Hungarian soldiers that I have seen in some book. Down it are rows of little buttons, but yet not buttons for they are made of the material itself.

That is what the Edwardian age recalls to me. In more serious moments it means the coming of the motor-car, with the chauffeurs of the Hall guests joining the hierarchy at the Lion, and soon a resident chauffeur in the village and the Greens spending most of their summers there. It recalls Green's racehorses and the win of a certain one in a very important race, and how all those in the know were on it at long odds to a man. The village won its first easy money, and who am I to moralize? I like a bet myself, if only on the Derby. And yet I cannot tell. That money came easily but maybe it was the dearest that many people bought.

One other thing that I associate with the entry of the Edwardian era is the coming of tomatoes. They were brought to the village by that hawker who came from Rockland with fish, and I believe the original price was sixpence a pound, which was a lot of money for those days and put them out of the reach of most people. There was a prejudice against them too, for it was said that they caused cancer. When I was first given a taste of one, I found it very unpalatable, but the common village way of eating them was to cut them up with vinegar and pepper and salt.

I have harped sufficiently on the remoteness of Heathley and yet newspaper and other publicity must have been potent

and far-reaching, for with each fresh publication by the Harms-
worths and other enterprising publishers, new weeklies and
even monthly magazines made their appearance in William
Cash's window on Friday nights, although the only publica-
tions he bought were those that had been previously ordered.
Even the swindlers managed somehow to lure us into their
schemes. I do not allude to that spate of catch-penny competitions that appeared in so many weeklies at about that time,
but to schemes that were tried on us through the post. How
our names were obtained I do not know, unless it was through
the electoral roll. But my experience has always been this.
Some say that if rogues turned honest men and devoted their
ingenuity to legitimate aims, then the world would be a better
place. I prefer to say that if honest men in their pursuit of
ideals devoted to their quest the skill and pertinacity of the
rogues, then the same results would be more quickly achieved.
The children of light, in my experience, are always the easy
prey of the children of darkness.

Take something that happened when I was no more than ten
years old. A letter came from some London firm announcing
a competition. It was not too difficult and I persuaded my
mother to let me have a shot at it. Apparently my attempt was
correct for I was sent a delightful-looking miniature alarm
clock as a prize. Others in the village had received notice of
the same competition but nobody appeared to have entered
but myself. I remember that John Balfour had a notice about
it in the *Ouseland and Hareborough Times.*

So far, so good. But a few months later came another
letter announcing another competition with even better prizes.
Again I sent in a solution and again I was notified that I had
won—and this time a handsome watch. The watch was sent
by registered post but attached to its acceptance was a condition—that the winner should buy a solid silver chain. The
chain was said to be practically given away but John Balfour
took pains over his inquiries and it was reckoned afterwards
that the price paid for the chain was sufficient to pay for chain,
watch and clock, and still leave a profit for the instigators of
the scheme.

I could give other instances, though even now it amazes me
that a village like Heathley should have been thought worthy
of inclusion in the swindling schemes of London sharpers. Or
was it our assumed *naïveté* that made it not only worth their

trouble but put us high on their list of the gullible. Even the Spanish Prisoner swindle had made its appearance in Heathley when I was still a boy.

But let me end this long chapter with what I regard as the best example of art in roguery that I have ever encountered. My father had a sister, Anne, who married a man named Lindsay, and the couple went to Australia and there prospered. I believe their sheep-farm was one of the largest in the Dominion, but be that as it may, two of their sons came to England and France in the Great War, and when the war was over they came to the ancestral home and saw my father.

Two years later, just before my return from Egypt, a letter arrived from a firm of Melbourne solicitors. Mrs. Lindsay's daughter was coming to school in England, and would stay in the Old Country till her education was completed. But would my father, her uncle, act as her guardian during that time, and be responsible for her during her holidays from school. Naturally my father was delighted, but what worried him was that the firm—a very superior firm from the quality of its notepaper—required him to deposit with them the sum of two hundred pounds as a kind of bond.

When I saw that letter I thought there was something strange about that request for money. Surely it should have been the other way. If we were to have the expense of my cousin on her holidays at least for several years, then somebody should have advanced us two hundred pounds as a sign of good faith. The upshot was that the letter was shown to my solicitors, who instituted inquiries in Melbourne itself. No such firm of solicitors existed! The address in such bold type was an accommodation one, and the handsome notepaper must have been specially printed. And the strange thing was that the two nephews of my father never remembered to have mentioned him to a living soul outside their family!

I have often wondered how that swindle was set in motion. It was fortunate that I happened to be at home or I believe that my father would have parted with such money as he might have been able to raise. But though he often alluded to certain 'jolly scoundrels' I believe he was rather flattered that even the rogues should have thought him of sufficient importance, and possessed of the not inconsiderable sum of a couple of hundred pounds.

Postscript.

After the manuscript of this book was in the hands of the publishers—on Sunday, December 2nd of last year, to be exact—I had a tremendous thrill. As a boy I had never heard old Boddy sing either of his songs for I was too young to attend a harvest supper. My father apparently knew neither tunes nor words, while that one derisive line which the boys would sing to infuriate the old man was certainly a mere ghost or travesty of the original.

But on that Sunday I was listening as usual to Country Magazine, when a song was announced. A Norfolk folk-song, and that made me prick my ears. But when the title was, 'I've Lost My Spotted Cow' I was struck with such an ecstasy that I ran into the kitchen to give the news and warn every one to be a listener. When the song had ended I was wishing to hear it again, sung by an untrained voice in Norfolk dialect, and I wished I had known shorthand so that I might have taken down at least the words. But that was foolishness perhaps, and ingratitude, for the mere announcement of the name of that song was a something I shall as foolishly never forget. In one miraculous moment I was back in my young boyhood, and Boddy himself was alive again.

Chapter IV

· THE HOME FAMILY

I WAS to have six sisters. The births of some of them I can
recall, but not of all. Perhaps I recall distinctly the arrival
of only one of them. She was born on a Good Friday afternoon, and it did not strike me as in any way strange that my
father should have told me that Walter Addis wanted me to do
odd jobs for him at the closed shop. There I spent the day
and probably as happy a one as ever I spent, for it was always a
joy to rummage about in the hinterland of the shop in the dark
storehouse where innumerable things were heterogeneously
heaped, and my peculiar perquisite was always an orange or
two that had become slightly tainted. When I smell an orange
to-day it always brings back the boxes in the Addis shop.

After tea my duties concluded with a message of some sort
to the housekeeper at the Hall. The original housekeeper had
gone and her place had been taken by a Mrs. Emerton, who was
later to become a friend of my mother. Mrs. Emerton gave me
a huge slice of cake, and I can see it now, for it was the most
wonderful cake on which I have ever clapped eyes. Not only
was it a rich brown but in it were crystallized fruits, and I
imagine it must have been a special Easter creation by the
French chef. But that cake was far too good for me to eat.
I carried it carefully home and asked where my mother was.
When I was told she was upstairs, I ran up to her room and
there she was in bed. A curious scent was in the air and by her
was lying a tiny baby of whom nothing but the black hair was

visible. All the Homes had black or dark brown hair and brown eyes.

I remember my mother was startled at my sudden entry, and even annoyed. When I gave her the cake she kissed me and then let me look at what she said was my little sister.

It was strange that I should have had no sex knowledge as far as it affected humans, for I kept rabbits and would take my does to the buck. Even just before a baby was coming I had no idea that one was on the way. When at school word went round that So-and-so was going to have a baby, I had only the vaguest ideas of the processes by which that baby would arrive. I do not think I was even interested, for there were far too many things in life to interest me as it was. But I did somehow learn to associate the arrival of Granny Shaw with the coming of a baby. Granny we loved if only because in my father's absence and with my mother upstairs we could do much as we liked.

I suppose I should be about eleven years old when Mrs. Pardon instituted a kind of maternity nursing service in the village, or perhaps managed to include Heathley in a service functioning in West Breckland. I recall a bitterly cold morning in winter. My father had to be up and away elsewhere so my brother and I were sent to fetch the nurse—Atkinson, I think her name was—from the outskirts of Croxton, a village in the heaths to the north of Ouseland. It was still dark when we set off and I remember the cutting wind across the bare heath roads and how the pony stumbled now and again on the strewn flints. The last mile was along a lonely track and finally we came to a little farm-house among the woods. I remember the sweet face of that nurse, and that though even to us she was young, she had a curious disciplinary influence which kept us quiet about the house compared with the days of Granny Shaw. I remember that when she left us she went to another cottage in the village, and that she came to tea with us from time to time. Later she married a village man and as he left the parish we lost sight of her.

Looking back I seem to see the children of Heathley as healthy and abounding in life. I know that never once did the doctor attend a single one of us, except my fourth sister, who was called Lucy after our aunt. And I suppose our diet varied little—except perhaps on Sundays—from that of any village family. There would be thick slices of bread, spread generally with good beef or pork dripping. There would be an abundance of vegetables and gravy, and though our roly-polys and currant duffs had remarkably few raisins and currants, they had plenty of good home-grown suet. I think, too—and to-day the Radio Doctor has confirmed it—that the uuiversal practice of breast-feeding gave us the best of starts in life and there was an abundance of country air, and an encouragement to drink plenty of water.

As for the one call the doctor did make on us, that was to attend a bad case of scalding. Lucy was the tiniest toddler and on the low hob a pot of pork was simmering. What actually happened we did not know, but she must have pulled at the handle and the pot capsized. So shockingly were the legs scalded that she was not expected to recover, but she did, and with few ill effects.

But I recall that sister for something quite different. In those days several firms had begun to popularize cocoa, and in our local papers would appear invitations to write for free samples. As the cost would be only a halfpenny stamp, we children were occasionally allowed to take advantage of the offer, for the cocoa would be used for our evening cups. Now one evening when we children were alone in our room, Lucy was writing a post card, and I think she would be then about eight years old. I think, too, it was I who snatched the post card away to see what she had been so long in writing, for all that was needed was one's own name and address. What I read aloud made us all laugh with fiendish delight.

Dear Mr. Rowntree,
I hope you are well. I have a rabbit which I keep in a box. . . .

That is all I remember but there was very much more, including some family news. But children in their sudden unaccountable malices are rather like hens. For some time after that we might be at a meal, and then some one would whisper, 'Dear Mr. Rowntree', and we would all shriek with laughter—except Lucy who would generally burst into tears.

My father had his own medicinal principles, or so I call them for want of a better word. In the house was always a very large bottle containing enough for many doses of salts and senna. But most dreaded was the spring. I assure you that this is no plagiarism of *Nicholas Nickleby* nor had my father ever read that book, but each spring there was mixed a bowl of sulphur and treacle, and of a consistency so thick that it adhered to the tongue and palate like so much glue. Each of us at intervals of a day or two was dosed with that terrifying concoction till the bowl was empty. How my sisters managed to swallow their spoonfuls I do not know, but I would retch, and my father would holler, 'Darst ye!' with dire promise of what would happen unless I contrived to swallow the abominable mess. If, indeed, you take that Phiz picture of the scene in Squeers's classroom and substitute for the emaciated urchin in the foreground one much shorter and very chubby, then you have a true vision of myself. And that sulphur and treacle was followed up by something almost as bad. My father was a great believer in the medicinal properties of rhubarb in the spring, and as soon as our own was well enough grown, there would be a monstrous bowl of it on the breakfast and tea-tables, and we would have to eat a heaping plate of it with bread and scrape, as we knew thinly spread bread and butter.

To be finicky with one's food was never allowed. I, fresh from a pampered life with my aunt, had a lesson which was soon to be learned. For one thing I did not like gobbets of sheer fat, and only the pleadings of my mother let me have the favour of being given principally lean. Then in one unguarded moment I made a slip. We had gone to kill a pig for the Goddards of Brackford, and I had been taken as a special treat. After the pig had been hung up ready for the following morning's weighing, we went to the farm-house kitchen to have tea. Roast pork was being carved and when I was asked about fat, I said courteously that I liked fat, and I meant that I did like a little fat of pork, though of nothing else. But after that my father was perpetually reminding me of what I had said, and I think he went out of his way to give me the fattest pieces. In time I came to eat them resignedly, for if I had not, they would have appeared at every subsequent meal.

Take the matter of those lumps of suet dumpling which would appear as soggy masses in stews. Those I definitely could not eat, but my father refused to accept the plea that I had not grown up with them as the rest of us had. When, at the end of a certain dinner, that soggy mass remained on my plate, I was told that there would be no more food for me till it had gone, and I had already lost my pudding. So at tea I ate nothing, though my mother smuggled me a cake on my way to bed. I ate nothing for breakfast, and at dinner I was still confronting nothing but that dumpling. When I came home from school that afternoon my mother called me to the kitchen. I can see her now asking why I would not eat that pudding. But she believed what I told her and then she cooked me an egg.

'You eat it with the egg,' she told me, 'and you won't taste it.'

That was how I managed to get that dumpling down. When we all assembled later for the normal tea, my father asked where the dumpling was, and my mother said simply that I had eaten it. My father was triumphant. Nothing like hunger for curing a finicky stomach.

I do not know what the issue of that battle would have been if my mother had not intervened, but I think I should have lasted out a good few meals for I had always a strain of tremendous obstinacy, and once I had made up my mind to a thing it took an enormous deal to budge me. But thereafter when I was given that soggy dumpling I was ready for it, for I would mash it with my fork and so mix it with gravy and vegetable that it was hard to discern its taste.

Perhaps the greatest joy of us children when young was the coming of relatives. My mother had a stepbrother, own brother of the aunt who had brought me up, and he was Uncle Ted. He had a very close friend, also a Methodist, whom we knew as Uncle Frank, and those two would always spend some days with us in the summer. But it was their way of coming to Breckland from London that was so unusual, for they would invariably walk all the way, and solely because they enjoyed the sights and sounds of the countryside. Their method was to do most of the walking by night, and they would do the hundred miles in just over two days. In advance of their coming would arrive a huge box of groceries, biscuits, and sweets, but it was not entirely for that that we loved those two uncles. Children are naturally gregarious and it was wonderful to see them and listen to them, and to have them sitting in our Sunday pew at the chapel. Most of their days would be spent with my father, and I can still see vaguely what must have been a scorching summer afternoon, with my peeping into the forbidden parlour where the two uncles were having a nap, each with a handkerchief over his face to keep away the flies, and Uncle Ted making strange noises with his open mouth. Above all I recall how curious it was to hear someone calling our father and mother by their Christian names.

Of Aunt Honor I have spoken elsewhere, but for her we had no affection for she was rather impatient of children. But we loved most of all my father's youngest sister, Aunt Lucy, and her husband, Fred Church. There could never have been a sweeter face or one with more kindly eyes than that of my aunt. One memory is always very near at Christmas-time, the only Christmas of my life when I remember the coming of relatives. To modern tastes that memory of fifty years ago will sound both maudlin and rustic, but I remember there had been the usual family singing with the eldest of us taking our parts.

'Why don't you sing to us, Lucy?' asked my mother.

'But I couldn't,' she said. 'Besides, I haven't any music.'

'What do you want music for?' asked my father in his usual impatient way. 'You've got a voice, haven't you?'

So Aunt Lucy sang to us without accompaniment, and we children listened spell-bound. Her voice had no particular quality, but it was quiet and sweet and gentle as herself. The song she sang was one we had never heard before, a song called, I believe, *Daddy*.

> The day has been long without you, Daddy,
> You've been such a time away,
> And you're as tired of your work, Daddy,
> As I am tired of my play.
> But you've got me and I've got you
> So everything's all right. . . .

After that one singing we children must have had those words by heart, and later the music was bought for a sister and we heard it often, though never as we had heard it that Christmas night. It is the custom to sneer at the family singing and the ballads of the last Victorian years, but the sneers are ill-based and largely the perquisite of those whose roots have no English depth. As for my Aunt Lucy, she died a very few years ago and at a great age. To her I owe innumerable kindnesses, and yet whenever I recall her it is in that little parlour on that Christmas night, we children clustered round her knees, and our eyes never once leaving her face as she sang that homely song.

One other curious memory comes back from those

Victorian times, the appearance in the village of a dancing bear. The man who led it had a strange costume, and I remember particularly a conical shaped hat with a tall feather in it. We were vastly afraid of that bear and stood at a good distance to watch it as it performed a shuffling with its feet and a raising of its forepaws, while the man played on a sort of accordion that was slung round his waist. One of us was deputed to give him a penny and I can still see the uncanny whiteness of his teeth as he grimaced in gratitude and smiled.

I think I was ten years old when I first saw Norwich. My father was accustomed to go there from time to time to buy timber in the bulk and such other things as he might need for the numerous jobs on which he was always engaged, and one Saturday, for some reason that I have forgotten, he decided to take me with him. And ever since, the Norwich of fifty years ago has been for me the only Norwich. That, as I have said elsewhere, is folly of the worst, but yet again I do not know. Much as I admire the great civic improvements, its new buildings and the widening of its essential streets, it is in the older parts of the city that I now spend my hours when I visit it. Whether it is that I am seeking a lost youth I do not know, but I do know that I feel a strange unhappiness and even a disquiet when I emerge from the lanes and haunts that I knew as a boy and come out to the full light of a modern day.

That first visit was thrilling from the moment I woke on that far-off Saturday morning. There was the ride in the pony and cart to Harford Station, where the pony was left in the inn stable with a feed that we had brought and with an injunction to the man to remember a subsequent pail of water. There was the thrill of entering a train for the first time since I had left London to come to Brandon with my aunt. There was the crowded compartment, with my father at once engaging in talk with the other occupants, and myself with eyes glued to the window. There were the stops at stations, with more farmers and their wives, and at last there was the first sight of the city itself as we entered past Colman's works.

Prince of Wales Road was one long enchantment, with its shops and stalls. It must have been in autumn for my father bought a bag of Victoria plums, and he and I ate them as we walked towards the market. In that great market space were what seemed to me thousands of cattle, and others being driven through the streets by shouting men and boys belabouring their rumps with sticks. But my father went past the market and for an hour he called at various wood-yards and I know that he went into an ironmonger's shop which I dimly remember as Gunton's. Then we went to Spellman's ring on Castle Hill where the horses were sold, for horses were always my father's first love, and almost his ruin.

I remember the immense crowd of farmers who stood in a great ring while in the middle the attendants trotted the horses round. Then came an incident which I shall never forget. A huge cart-horse was being trotted round and the man called that it was a kicker. My father drew me back and just after that horse was well past us it gave a cow-kick with a hoof that seemed to me as large as a tray. That hoof went straight for the face of another small boy who stood with his father on the edge of the ring. So near did it go that there could not have been the width of a hand between face and hoof, and I remember the sudden silence and the gasp that went through the crowd, and how when the horse had passed men rushed forward, for that hoof would have smashed that face to something like pulp.

Next we went in search of dinner. The restaurant, between Castle Hill and the Market, was crowded with farmers and their families, but I remember we had roast beef, Yorkshire pudding, and vegetables. I can still see my plate, swimming in gravy, and in it green peas from a tin or else dried, for they were so hard that I had to mash them with my potatoes to get them to my mouth. Then my father took me to the Castle and we went through the museum with its vast collection of stuffed birds and animals. It was the picture gallery that interested me most. Those were the first real pictures I had ever seen, and I could have spent the rest of the afternoon among the water-colours. It was that afternoon that made me determine to be a painter. That very next week I bought a penny drawing-book and began my career with an attempt to sketch our chapel. I found that book and that sketch only a few years ago. It was not bad as the line drawing of a small boy, and I remember that just as I had finished it, William Cash happened to stroll by. He walked back in his slow, aloof way and had a look at it. His nod was non-committal and rather damped my ardour.

After that we looked at the shops with my father making various purchases, and then we had to catch the late afternoon train. Soon after six o'clock we were home again. I cannot remember what I brought my mother but it must have been something, for whenever there was an occasion on which we children had a few coppers to spend, something was set aside for a present to our mother. But now I come to think of it, I know what I did buy that famous day. It was a small piece of crested china—Goss as we used to call it—that was to stand for years on the corner whatnot in the parlour with the Wedgwood and the rest of my mother's treasures.

So much for what was up to then the greatest day of my life. The following autumn there was to come an even greater. I have said that as a return for my labour I was always promised a trip to Yarmouth. The occasion was to present itself, if in an unusual way. Many years later I made of that day a short story, of which the title might have been either *A Trip to Yarmouth* or *The Copper Kettle*. As I now relate it, every word and happening is implicitly true, and I myself shall live again the events of that day as if it were only as yesterday.

My sister died six years ago and when she was staying with me for the last time, we talked about that day at Yarmouth. As I wanted at the time to make a story from it, I induced her to give me the ending from her own point of view, as she remembered it.

There was a man from whom my father had expectations of valuable work, and he had a small daughter whom we will call Emily, and she was of the age of my eldest sister. Now I am of the opinion that it was to this man—Harper, shall we say, by name—that my father had mentioned in his usual airy way something about a trip to Yarmouth, and Harper had at once asked if Emily could make one of the party. Maybe Harper even thought the trip had been definitely arranged, but at any rate my father found that the trip now had to be taken. The reasons given may sound strange, but I can assure you that the last thing in the world my father wished was to take his whole family to Yarmouth. Though he was fond of his children and would nurse and fondle the youngest in the house itself, he would never be seen with us abroad. Our small steps were too slow for his impatient strides. I never even knew him accompany my mother as far as the chapel.

I was in the house that evening when he made the suggestion
to my mother. My ears were pricked at once and I was on
tenterhooks till she had fallen in with his idea. Then when she
had committed herself, my father introduced the subject of
Emily Harper. She would be no trouble, he said, and the two
eldest girls could look after her. My mother shook her head.
Maybe she knew more about Emily Harper than he and I, but
she did hint that only children were often spoilt.

'She'll be no worry,' my father told her confidently. 'I'll
keep an eye on her myself.'

As far as he was concerned everything was then settled, but
my mother had to look farther ahead. What about food? There
was myself and three sisters and another sister who could only
just toddle, and there would be the parents and Emily Harper.
That would mean preparation and a heavy load to carry. Most
of that load would be for me and my father, for she would
have the baby. That made my father pause, and then as quickly
he had a solution. There were plenty of restaurants at Yarmouth and we could get our midday meal in one of them.
When my mother protested that the cost would be too great,
my father laughed. He was used to driving bargains and he'd
take care not to be swindled by any restaurant proprietor in
Yarmouth. All that needed to be carried then was a little
something for our teas.

I know now that there were other things my mother would
have liked to discuss beforehand, but she kept them to herself.
For my father was a man of queer temper who hated, like
myself, to be turned from a path he had chosen. His rages
righteous and otherwise, were terrifying things, and what
were more frightening still were his fits of reserve, as when he
was brooding over some grievance. And so everything was
arranged and at last the great day came. Harper drove us all
to Harford Station in his wagonette and was to meet us in
the evening. It was a magnificent day of early autumn.
Harvest had been good and we had all been given small sums
to spend. Emily Harper had a shilling, beyond what was
needed for a spade and bucket, and I remember that when she
began pestering my mother about ways of spending it, she
was told that the best thing to do was to buy something
sensible that she could keep.

It was an excursion train, and the full return fare no
more than one and threepence for the long journey. We

were lucky enough to get an empty compartment to ourselves.

'Don't you worry about Emily,' my father told Harper. 'I'll look after her myself.'

In the train we clustered round the windows and my father pointed out the countryside, and at each station, much to my mother's secret disgust, he would be looking out of the window to hail any one of his innumerable acquaintances. And so to Norwich and then on to Yarmouth. As we neared the sea the excitement was unbearable. Then at last we did see it, and soon the brakes began to grind. I was given the big basket and my eldest sister—then about nine—was given the smaller, and was told to share with my second sister the responsibility for Emily

The packed train emptied itself and we at last emerged at the street. We began asking about spades and buckets, so my father told us to follow him and off he went. When we managed to find him he was outside a shop that displayed an incredible number of spades and buckets, and while we waited, he went into the shop and bargained with the woman. It was while he was there that we caught sight of the little copper kettle.

How can I describe it? Only perhaps through the eyes of my mother, though I knew that it was a perfect kettle in miniature, and so quaint and homely that it made one smile.

'What a lovely little kettle!' my mother said. 'Wouldn't I love it polished on the mantelpiece. It would go beautifully with the candlesticks.'

'May I have it, mother?' asked my eldest sister.

'No, dear. I'm afraid it would cost too much money,' she was told.

'May I have it?' asked Emily.

'We'll see, dear. Perhaps if it's not too much money. But we'll see.'

When my father came out with the spades and buckets, my mother mentioned the matter. Father called the woman out.

'How much do you want for that little old kittle?'

'It's a shilling,' she said.

'A shilling!' my father said in horror. 'What you mean is sixpence.'

She shook her head, but a smile accompanied it. Perhaps he knew he would get it at his price and as we did not want to carry even so small a thing as that kettle with us all day, we made our way towards the beach. We went through the narrow Yarmouth rows and then at last there was the open sea. My mother sat with the baby, her back resting against a groyne, and we children paddled and made sand castles, and every now and again we would find a shell or treasure and run to exhibit it to mother. Then Emily insisted on venturing too far out, and an oncoming wave wetted her frock and she began to cry noisily.

By the time she was quietened my father had lost his temper and but for my mother's intervention I think he would have shaken her. But in any case he was impatient of staying so long in one place and, telling mother he would not be long, he went off to see the sights. As the morning drew on, we children became ravenously hungry, for we had breakfasted soon after six o'clock, and I was sent to find my father. I found him laughing at the photographers' stand where people were having photographs taken, their heads through the holes that took the place of the heads of painted donkeys and various grotesques. I enjoyed that myself, but when I gave him mother's message he told me to go back and he would see about dinner himself.

I think he had forgotten all about it, but back I went and we children went on playing. The baby was fed with rusks, and then hunger was becoming unbearable, especially at the sight of other people eating their meals. What seemed like hours went by and then at last my father appeared. He was carrying some parcels.

'I wasn't going to pay the price them jolly rogues was askin',' he told us in broad Norfolk, and for the information of every one around. 'Get you the children sat down, mother, and we'll have a dinner in spite o' them jolly rascals.'

Never shall I forget that meal. There were loaves of bread, a tin of corned beef and a pot of pickles, and there was enough for all. Perhaps because my mother ate little. It irked her to eat in front of so many people who would stare at my father's hearty laughs, and she was longing for a cup of tea. Then there came a minor disaster and towards the very end of the meal. Emily had been eating more slowly than the rest of us, and what she did was to drop on the sand a slice of bread and beef that my father handed her. Once more she began to blubber, and he had to give her his own last slice to quieten her. I am positive once more that he would have shaken her.

'Be quiet, you little hussy, do!' was what he did tell her, and that was all. Harper and his work must have been in his mind, for my father was in no position to quarrel with his living.

After the meal he had a nap while we children went on with our play. I think it must have been at about three o'clock when he woke, and then he was off again with another assurance that he would be back before long, and we were not to move from where we were. Years afterwards I managed to get from him where he went. As a young man in London he had been passionately fond of the Christy and the Moore and Burgess Minstrels, and that afternoon he spent an hour or two with a concert-party.

But before he had been gone half an hour, the ominous clouds rolled up. There were rumbles of distant thunder, and if there was anything of which my mother was terrified, it was a thunderstorm, or tempest, as we called it. At home she would crouch beneath the stairs till it had passed, and it always left her with a blinding headache—a something that I have inherited. I remember she got us round her like a hen gathering her chicks and then as the first drops of rain began to fall, a man saw her plight and came to us. The beach crowd had already scattered and he helped us to the shelter beneath one of the piers, and there we crouched while the rain tore down and the storm was in full blast.

Then at long last the sky began to clear. The rain mercifully stopped and I was sent to find my father. I forget where I met him but even to me he was voluble with excuses. When my mother began quietly to upbraid him, he lost his temper as a man will often do who knows himself in the wrong and lacks the moral courage to acknowledge the fact. What did she expect him to do, he demanded. Go through that rain with no coat and get wet to the skin? And what were we all doing sitting there, when the train left in another half-hour. Off we trooped and the sun was now shining again. By chance we went by the way we had come, and my father went on ahead in the grip of one of those frightening reserves. Then as we came to the shop, there was that little copper kettle still in the window. Emily had spent only a penny or so on an ice-cream, so my mother called my father back. Would he buy the kettle for Emily.

He bought it, but the paying of even the ninepence was no improvement to his temper. Then when he handed it to Emily, she said she didn't want it!

'Don't want it?' He glared at her. 'Why'd you make me buy it then, you little hussy?'

'You have it, dear,' my mother told her gently. 'It'll be lovely for a doll's tea-party.'

'Do you want it or do you not!' demanded my father fiercely.

Then Emily began to blubber, and in a fit of furious rage he hurled the kettle from him.

'Come along, together. Are we goin' to catch that train or are we not?'

We moved off, he striding ahead. I suddenly slipped back and retrieved that copper kettle from the gutter where it had fallen. As I ran I wiped its mud on my jacket and then slipped it under my shirt.

Once more we were lucky to have a compartment to ourselves, and when the train started we ate our tea. It was a cup of tea for which my mother would have given everything, for she had one of her headaches. My father would eat nothing but sat in his corner, and we were kept quiet as mice. What he must have been thinking was that Emily would be sure to tell tales to her father, and that would mean the end of Harper's work.

So that wretched journey went on. Then I surreptitiously got out the little kettle and began wiping the mud from it and polishing it again. It was slightly dented where it had fallen, and as I was wondering how to remove the dent, my father caught sight of me.

'What's that you've got there?'

His voice had an ominous calm, but mercifully I was saved. The train had stopped at a station and was about to move off again when a man came hurrying up. He had a small boy with him, and the two entered our compartment just in time.

'A narrow squeak,' the man said, as he took the only available seat.

'I think we can make room for your little boy to sit down,' my mother said.

'Don't you worry, ma'am,' the man told her. 'Stand you agin that door, Herbert. We're only goin' as far as Ouseland.'

The train gathered speed, and then suddenly an amazing thing happened. My father fairly leapt across that compartment. He had that boy by the jacket collar and he flung him back. Then he opened the window and closed the door against which the boy had been leaning. The boy's father gasped.

'That door was open?'

The door *had* been open. The least pressure against it and the boy would have fallen on the line. But for my father's ill-humour that had kept us quiet on our seats, one of us must have fallen long before.

The man's face was white. I can see him now, shaking my father's hand again and again.

"Anything I can ever do for you, do you let me know. I reckon you saved his life.'

'I don't know,' my father said deprecatingly. 'I don't know about that, neighbour. But I reckon he might have been good-tidy hurt.'

The compartment had miraculously changed, and so had my father. Once more the blood ran genially through his veins. He could see our awe at his saving of that boy. Even my mother spoke words of gratitude, and in his ears were the man's praise and thanks. But my eldest sister was perhaps the happiest of all. I had passed her the little copper kettle, and she was happily hugging it. Then the sound of a blubber from Emily disturbed my father's talk with the man.

'What's a-matter now?' he asked, but genially.

'I want my kettle,' blubbered Emily.

'Well, have your kettle,' he told her. 'I bowt it for you, didn't I?'

So Emily triumphantly took the kettle, and then the train slowed for Harford Station. To the sound of the man's repeated thanks we made our way to the road where Harper was waiting with the wagonette. An enormous smile of gratitude was on his face as Emily ran to him.

'Well, and how have my little old woman enjoyed herself?'

'Ever so, father,' she said. 'And look what I've got!'

'Well, well,' he said. 'If that ain't the rummest little kittle ever I seed.'

Home we drove and when Harper dropped us at our house he expressed his warmest thanks.

'There ain't nothin' to thank me for,' my father told him.

'She weren't no trouble. A score like her wouldn't have worried me.'

And as Harper drove away, with Emily clutching that little copper kettle, my sister began to cry gently to herself.

'What is it, dear?' my mother asked.

'It was *my* kettle,' she was told fiercely. 'Michael gave it me.'

'Sh!' my mother told her, for we were still in earshot of my father. But Hilda remembered that she had frowned and shaken her head with a queer perplexity. In that perplexity was perhaps all the strange shiftings of a day that had almost gone. A queer day, sunny and stormy, soothing and worrying, happy and frightening, bright and discoloured, and all of it a dimly remembered something that merged into a coming home. And there, now also going and clutched in Emily's hands as a kind of symbol, was that quaint wee kettle that had somehow been the day itself.

Chapter V

THE GREAT ADVENTURE

I MUST warn a reader of *God and the Rabbit* that he will find this chapter somewhat familiar. But the events as there related were only in part true autobiography. They were the adaptations of a novelist made to fit the circumstances and environment of a family which, however truly drawn, was nevertheless fictitious. The story as here given is implicitly true. There is no intrusion of fiction, no over-emphasis, and, above all, no romantic colouring. What I remember I have written, and no more.

On account of my extraordinary upbringing with my aunt I was rather a precocious child. I recall little of my private schooling, but I do know that I could read at the age of four, and that at seven years I knew by heart whole pages of the only books I was allowed to read—a picture Bible, Bunyan's *Pilgrim's Progress* and Josephus's *History of the Jews*. That I possessed a most astounding memory was also true, though I take no more credit for that than if I had received the gift of uncanny hearing. It is a gift that has now almost gone, but up to quite recent times it was still with me, and I could boast that if one mentioned to me a trisyllabled word from any of the better-known plays of Shakespeare, I would give the context and, in some cases, most of the page. But I can still remember things that most people would have forgotten, and those plays of Shakespeare that we read at school I can still say off by heart.

5

But be all that as it may, when I attended the school of my native village, John Balfour was soon to become aware that after years of geese and unchanging ugly ducklings, he had come upon a queer sort of swan. It was he who suggested to my mother that I should have private coaching, with the prophecy that one day I should become Lord Mayor of London! But in that crowded village school with its stolidities, its plodders, its louts and hobbledehoys, there was never any singling out of myself, nor was any favour shown. John Balfour was far too harassed a man, and he allowed himself no fatal weakening of discipline. Indeed I was far from a favourite. Adventurous always, I seemed as always to collide with mischief, and when I was designedly mischievous I was so with a subtlety.

There was an occasion, for instance, when we were having a lesson in arithmetic. A sum which we had been shown some days before was put on the board and we were left to do it. As soon as I had written down the answer I was busy at my drawing. When John Balfour returned and asked for our answers, I was the only one who had that sum right.

'Give me your slate,' he said, 'and I'll write your method on the blackboard.'

A moment later he was calling me to the front.

'What's this?'

This was the fact that I'd remembered the answer and as I couldn't be bothered with working the sum out, I'd put down some sort of gibberish and the answer at the bottom of it. His face, always red, went purple beneath the ruddy beard, and with his open hand he gave me a clout on the ear that landed me yards away.

Then there was the occasion when he asked me if I had been talking.

'Yes, sir,' I said.

'What did you say?'

That I refused to divulge, so he put the question to the boy whom my remark had apparently convulsed. That boy—a boy named Stewart from Wortley—let me down.

'Please, sir, he said that Old John was gettin' a rare pod[1] on him.'

John, face flaming, strode towards me, and once more, before I could dodge, I felt the hand of justice.

[1] Stomach.

I relate those things because never did John Balfour allow my mischief or thoughtlessness to harm what he thought to be my future prospects, and whatever the day had been, I was welcomed that evening at his house. I know that I hated those lessons especially on summer evenings, but I remember very little of them, and doubtless because I hated them so much. All indeed that comes clearly from my schooldays is the endless drawing on my slate whenever I could steal a minute. By me there sat for some months a boy named Meek, whose father was a team-man. He would draw profile heads of horses and nothing else, though the reins and blinkers would be differently ornamented. I, engrossed for months in *Westward Ho!* and *The Rise of the Dutch Republic* specialized in Spanish warriors in mail and morion, and Spanish galleons.

And then when I was ten years old, something happened. Our papers announced and John Balfour received official word that the County was granting scholarships from primary schools to grammar and secondary schools. The scholarships—I believe there were to be a hundred and twenty of them in that first year—were open to all Norfolk. John Balfour came at once to see my parents.

It was my mother who pointed out the hopelessness of it as far as I was concerned. There were enough outstanding children in Norwich alone to carry off all those scholarships, and if one took into account the schools of all the towns, what chance could be stood by a boy from a little village school. I think John Balfour was in his heart of hearts of the same opinion, and yet he was not the sort to throw in his hand. In any case the upshot was that private lessons, much to my disgust, were increased, and for a long time after that I really had to work. There were lessons in advanced arithmetic, history, grammar, and geography, with text-books of his own that he lent me. Thanks to them I managed to avoid most of my normal household duties, and many a holiday afternoon I spent on the heaths, my back against a pine-tree, perhaps, or roaming heaths and brecks as soon as I knew by heart the lesson for a night.

At last the great day came. I was not in the least excited, and because I had no means of perceiving the day's implications. But John Balfour and my mother burdened me with final advice and instructions, and carrying my lunch and the

official papers I set off to catch the quarter past nine one
Saturday morning at Wortley Station. It was the first time
I had gone by train to Ouseland, and by train alone, so I
snuggled into my corner seat and prepared to look at the
unfamiliar countryside. Then a voice called to me.

In that compartment was a man with his son, a boy of my
own age or rather older. He was a short, fat man, wearing a
dark suit. A handsome chain was across his middle and on
his little finger a gold ring, and it flashed when he twirled
back his florid moustache. The boy was much better clad
than myself, even though I was wearing my Sunday clothes.
His boots were not hobnailed and he was wearing a starched
collar *outside* his jacket. Mine was a collar of celluloid.

'You, boy! Are you goin' to Ouseland?'

I said I was, even if I said it warily. My mother had warned
me against strangers.

Next he asked me my name and where I came from and
said he thought he knew my father.

'I suppose you're goin' up for this scholarship examination?'

I said I was.

'How do you reckon you're goin' to get on?'

I said I didn't know; probably the most accurate answer
I've ever given.

'Know your history?'

I said I'd read the two books the master had lent me.

'Read two books, have you?' he said, and twirled his
moustache. 'Well, what's the date of the Battle of Agincourt?'

John Balfour always said that dates mattered little compared
with the facts of history, but I knew I ought to know that
date. Was it fifteen-fourteen or fourteen-fifteen? I chose the
former. The pompous little man gave a snort.

'Wrong,' he told me fiercely. 'Leonard, what's the date of
the Battle of Agincourt?'

'Fourteen-fifteen, father.'

'There you are,' he told me. 'And what's the date of Magna
Carta?'

That was altogether beyond me.

'Leonard, what's the date of Magna Carta?'

'Twelve-fifteen, father.'

'Right,' he said. He gave his moustache another twirl and

his lip curled as he turned again to me. 'And if you don't know no more about geography and arithmetic than you do about history, the best thing you can do is to slip off back home to Heathley.'

I was at that moment of the same opinion, and when we reached Ouseland and I saw the numbers of children who got off that train, I was even more sure of it. Most of them were much taller than I, and some were accompanied by their parents, but all at once I had not the faintest intention of taking the advice of the complacent parent of my compartment, and I followed on the heels of the crowd. The school at Ouseland rather overawed me. To me it was almost a palace after the Heathley school, but before there was time to do more than hand in the official papers, the arithmetic examination was at hand.

Mathematics have never been my strong point, and how I fared that day I do not know, for I was not aware until after that first examination that we were permitted to take away our question papers. After arithmetic came dictation, and that caused me no alarms. To end the morning came grammar and composition.

Did ever a boy have such amazing luck?—not that I was to feel a confidence. What I did feel was the joy of being able to write and write, and about the things that I liked. The grammar paper had plenty of analysis and parsing, and that was something in which I had long revelled, for when I had become proficient John Balfour had begun a kind of game in which he would try to catch me out with trick sentences. As for the Essay or Composition, that was handed to me on a gold salver.

Which would you rather be if you had the choice: a doctor, a police-man, or a shepherd? Give your reasons.

Needless to say I chose the shepherd. I brought in the shepherd boy David, and the shepherd boy from *Pilgrim's Progress* and the song he sang. I gave an account of a Heathley shepherd's life and, indeed I was just getting well into the subject when the supervisor announced that in two minutes the papers would be collected. What I did then was what John Balfour had told me: I put in a bracket the words— *No time to finish*—and left it at that.

There was a special room in which we could eat our

dinners, though most of the candidates went out. Then in the afternoon came history, and I remember there was no question involving dates. Geography came next and I had a fine chance of doing some map drawing of which I was very fond. Then came an oral examination that lasted about ten minutes. My examiner was a man with a short black beard, and he had a reassuring way with him. He asked me what I had read and all I can think now is that the miscellaneous reading that I claimed must have left him somewhat incredulous. He also asked me what I wanted to be when I grew up, and I said a painter.

'An artist?'

'No, sir. A painter,' I said.

'What sort of painter?'

'The sort that paints pictures like those in the Museum at Norwich,' I said, and that's all that I remember. But next I had to go to a kind of clerk who handed me five shillings and sixpence! That was ninepence a mile for horse hire to get me to Wortley Station and back; eighteenpence for lunch and the rest railway fare. Then when I came out of the school I had nowhere to go, so I made my way back to the railway station. There a comic paper caught my eye on the bookstall, so I bought it out of the coppers I had been given for eventualities, and read it by the waiting-room fire till my train at last came in.

It was pitch dark when I got to Wortley Station, but I was lucky enough to get a ride. I ran home from where I was set down and burst into the house with my five and sixpence. That was for me the miracle of that day, that I had had an outing and been paid handsomely for it. As the unexpected ride had brought me home earlier than foreseen, I was sent to report to John Balfour while my meal was warmed up.

John Balfour made me go through every paper and every question I had answered, and that inquiry consisted either of reproachful clickings of the tongue or chucklings and crowings. I remember he was exasperated that I should not have differentiated between painters and artists, but at the end he gave me a pat on the head and said there was no use crying over spilt milk and the only thing to do was wait for the few weeks till the results came out.

When I got back home, my father was there and he and my mother began questioning me. I was far from happy about how I had done, and when I remembered mistakes I had made, my father began to upbraid me. My mother defended me like a tigress.

'Don't talk to the boy like that,' she said. 'He's done his best and that's all that any one could do. He never did stand a chance—we all knew that. And the money he brought home is all going in his money-box.'

Then I remembered the man in the train, and never have I seen my father so furious as when I'd described him.

'I know him,' he said. 'Chapman. That's his name. A rare botty[1] little old fusser.' He clenched his fist. 'If I run across him next time I'm at Hareborough, I'll give him a piece of my mind he won't forget.'

Even my mother was indignant, and there ended that notable day. For twelve hours I had been something of a hero. Next morning I was normal again, though for some weeks I rejoiced at the absence of private lessons.

On a hot afternoon of early summer my mother was dozing in our little living-room when there came a knock at the door. Without waiting for a call, John Balfour looked in, and then he seized my mother's two hands and began shaking them, and though his face was wreathed in smiles, his eyes were puckering as if he were going to cry.

'Why, whatever's the matter?' she asked him.

'Haven't you heard!'

She shook her head, and then something came to her.

'You don't mean that Michael's won a scholarship?'

But that was what it was. On our mantelpiece was a letter that had come that morning for my father, and, thinking it was a bill, my mother had left it till his return home at evening. Now she and John Balfour opened the letter, and sure enough there was the official notification. He had seen the list of successful candidates that afternoon in the *Eastern Daily Press*.

I remember very little else that happened that day. I gave myself no airs and I was not very excited, for I had not the faintest idea what it would be like to go to another school. I do remember that when my father remarked proudly that I was near the top of the list, I pointed out that that was because the names were in alphabetical order. Actually my position was somewhere in the middle.

[1] Self-important.

'Give you me that paper again, mother,' my father suddenly said. 'I want to see if that botty little Chapman's boy have got a scholarship too.'

He ran his eye down the list, and frowned.

'That's funny. I can't find the name nowhere.'

But it wasn't funny really, for the name wasn't there!

I think that feat of mine was the biggest sensation Heathley had had for years. That a village boy should for the first time in its history be going to another school was an astounding thing. But a good few shook their heads, for one of the quickest roads to unpopularity is to hitch your wagon to a star. Even among our friends were many who advised most strongly against my attending a school so famous as the old grammar school at Ouseland. What would do me far more good, and fit me more for a job as a clerk, was the Commercial School at Windley, and there too I should feel much more at home. Or there was a little grammar school of a much more modern foundation at Saham, near Hareborough, where quite a lot of the sons of local tradesmen went.

But my mother had other views. Even in my youngest days I often heard her tell us something she must have heard from her own mother, that if in life you were fated to be a crossing-sweeper, then you should make up your mind to be the best crossing-sweeper in the street. So after she had received all the prospectuses of the various schools, she sought the advice of the Reverend John Pardon. The scholarship was sufficient to pay the fees at Ouseland and the railway fare, but left nothing for eventualities as a cheaper school would have done. Nevertheless, he too was of the opinion that Ouseland was the one and only school, and worth the sacrifices entailed. Indeed he made no bones about stating that I was exceedingly lucky to have the chance of attending such a school. But there was one difficulty, though not an insuperable one. Such day boys as came from neighbouring towns ate lunch with the boarders at a charge of a shilling a day, and that was a sum beyond my parents' means.

Now John Pardon knew well the Reverend Benjamin Reed, the head master of Ouseland, for occasionally he would preach in Heathley church, and he proposed to my mother that he should see the head master and make the financial position perfectly clear. There were other difficulties which could be smoothed out at the same time, but he did strongly advise that I should take the Modern side, which meant German and French as against Latin and French, with possibly Greek. To that my mother could only gratefully agree, but that non-learning of Latin was to change for the infinite better the whole current of my life, and not because of the German that took its place.

The weeks went by and then just before the opening of term, my mother and I were summoned to Ouseland to interview the head master. Never shall I forget my first sight of that august figure when we chanced to meet him outside the schoolhouse on that lovely September morning. He was tallish and sparely built; reddish of face and with a heavy black moustache, but the most noticeable thing about him were the kindly looking wrinkles at the corners of his eyes, though most of my school life was to see in them things far remote from kindliness. His linen seemed dazzlingly white and his silk topper shone in the morning sun, and he raised it to my mother with the same flourish he would have bestowed on a paying parent.

'Mrs. Home, is it?'

I forget what my mother said, but I know I pulled off my cap. He gave me a quick searching look and then escorted us to his study. My mother received a list of books which could be obtained free in the town, and the name of the shop that supplied school caps and ties. When the business was over there was an impressive minute that made me shiver in my shoes. Old Benn, as I was to come to know him, gave me a grim look.

'I expect to meet with mischief in my scholars, Mrs. Home, and I know how to cope with it. But one thing I never forgive—a boy who tells me a lie.'

All my life I remembered that grim moment, just as my mother remembered and was grateful for the exquisite courtesy of a man in whose eyes she was patently no more than a humble woman of the Breckland countryside. But Old Benn advised us too to look round the school itself, and this we then did. George Mower, caretaker and professional, escorted us round, and I know that I was overawed. But George unbent when he knew who we were, for he had often played cricket with my father.

But when we called at the shops, my mother was dismayed

at the prices of clothes such as I should have to wear. But instead of letting her buy a cheap satchel for my books, the shopkeeper advised her to have a stout leather one, and whatever the price she paid, it was a bargain, for my youngest sister was using that same satchel till almost twenty years later, and I believe that then it was passed to a nephew. Many a hundred miles did I carry it and packed to capacity with books and lunch, and never once did it need a repair.

We went home by the midday train—the half-arter twelve as we knew it at Heathley—and I remember that my mother warned me strictly that on no account was I to let my father know the cost of the things she had bought. How the money was found I do not know. Not by my father, for only on very rare occasions had he money to spare for me, but it must have been my mother who denied herself this and that.

I think my father was inordinately proud of having a son at Ouseland Grammar School, but that pride never showed itself in any sacrifice. Indeed, when financial crises arose he would be wondering if it were not time for me to be leaving school and earning a living. It was on such occasions that my mother would show a rare anger. My scholarship was for three years, and three years I was going to stay, and she would speak with such a chill finality that my father would hesitate to argue the point.

The only other things that happened in those few days before my departure for Ouseland were the arrival of a railway season-ticket, and the gift to me of a Bible and *Hymns Ancient and Modern* by the Reverend. John Balfour and Walter Addis both inspected my books, and I think John Balfour must somehow have envied me my opportunities. When I think of him now and all I owed and the little I was able to repay, there is a shame for the incredible greatness of the one and the pitiful poverty of the other. But it is high time, as they say, to leave this brief interlude and get back to the family again.

From that family I was now to be somewhat apart. Since my school clothes had to be donned on rising, there was no more fetching of horses or feeding of bullocks and pigs, and by half-past eight I would be away and gone. Then at night it would often be nearly seven o'clock when I reached home and the youngest of my sisters would be in bed. As for the two that might still be up, I would infuriate them by glancing meaningly at the clock, for my mother would often catch the gesture and interpret it as a sign that my homework needed concentration, though often it had already been done or scamped, and all I was wanting was to get back to some favourite book.

Chapter VI

THE HOME FAMILY—*continued*

LIKE many people I think that of all the senses that of smell
most easily recalls the past. When I smell a rose I invariably
remember the moss roses of our Heathley gardens, and the
scent of sweet briar brings back a memory even more remote,
of a little country lane in Fenwold when, as a very small boy,
I lived there for a time with my aunt. Most near is the scent
of clean wheat straw, which brings back the heat of an August
noon when in a pause from the thatching we sat on the dry
straw to eat our midday meal.

At the front of our house were a few clumps of chrysanthemums. They were of no particular quality but my mother
liked them for cutting and my father and I would use them
for Sunday buttonholes when all other flowers had gone. I
always loved their scent which was somehow the scent of home,
for in late autumn one clings more closely to a house itself, and
with the dark nights that house acquires a new significance.

My eldest sister was in Malta at the outbreak of the Great
War and it had to be many months before she left it. On
that first Christmas Day she was walking through a street in
Valetta, and, with the strangeness of distance, was feeling no
special homesickness. And then suddenly she caught a
familiar smell, and there at an open window was a pot of
chrysanthemums. In a moment the village was overwhelm-
ingly back and, as she put it, she sat on the steps of that little
house and cried her eyes out.

A certain peculiar whiff from a wood fire will take me suddenly to the desert, and a Bedouin encampment and a dung fire. Just before this present war I was working with my gardener when I caught such a whiff and in a moment was back among the sand and flies and heat. A moment or two of nostalgia and day-dreaming and then I wondered what had brought those memories back. It was then that I noticed that my man had lighted his pipe!

I have said that I have no wish to regain a lost youth, and yet that is scarcely true. That one of the world's six most notable plots wherein a man becomes himself as a child and still retains his older experience appeals to me if only for one reason. Not in order that I should be able to control my destiny, for I have no quarrel with that, but that I could confront my father with quiet logic and argument when called before him for judgment on some particular escapade. For his discipline was Spartan in its severity and took little heed of degrees of guilt or punishments to fit a crime. His was the stick or whip, laid on with the fervour of indignation or wrath. And yet I know that if he had been accused of too strict a discipline he would have been just as wrathful or indignant. After all, we were treated as he himself had been treated, and he would have added the reminder about the spared rod and the spoilt child.

But there was a capriciousness about his judgments that made the few moments before a decision very much of a mental strain for the culprit. I had learned never to tell him a lie, if only because a frank confession often condoned a crime. And yet I could never be certain. And what was far more exasperating was that when one told the truth and insisted on innocence, he occasionally refused to believe. But I should make it clear that in such matters he differed little from other village fathers. Nor did the punishments apply to my sisters. Only in the rarest cases were they punished by him, and I have often heard my mother stoutly defending them against his wrath and insisting that their punishment was her province.

As an example of that capriciousness let me take the Sunday when I looked down from the branches of an apple tree and saw my father contemplating me from beneath. When he had had his fill of the sight of the paralysed me, he walked away. Terror filled my young soul as I made my own way home, for I had been stealing apples, and on the Sabbath, and climbing a tree in my Sunday clothes. Then at last I was called into the parlour.

'That was William Cash's tree you were up,' he said to me: part question, part indictment.

'Yes, father.'

He grunted once or twice, then nodded.

'Well, I shan't punish you this time. You can go.'

There had been an ironical smile with that dismissal, and I knew that my amazing discharge had been due to the fact that at that time he and William Cash were on terms of the most bitter enmity.

When I look back at the crimes for which I was punished, I see them as no more than pranks that had little devilry. Take the case of Porky Carman's barrow. Even my father would remark how surly that old roadman was, even if he was a brother Methodist. One day when I had business along the Shopleigh Road old Carman threatened to report me to my father for throwing a stone at a rabbit, and on my return he was working round a bend of the lane with his barrow well out of sight and by it a pot of tar and a brush. So I printed a neat—PORKY CARMAN—on the barrow side, and then tarred the ends of the handles. Though you may not believe me—and my father certainly did not—I assure you that I tarred those handles because handling had stripped them of paint. They somehow offended my artistic and utilitarian sense and never for a moment did it occur to me that Porky would not see the tar before his fingers closed round it. There, in any case, is something I should like now to argue with my father.

Then there was the dog belonging to West of the Eagle. It would roam our end of the village and my father would hurl a stick at it when he found it on his garden. No one grumbled more than he at that dog, and yet when I tried an experiment which ensured that it should never bother us again, I received one of the thrashings of my life. All I did was to tempt the dog to come up to me when I saw him on our garden, and then I tied an empty biscuit tin to his tail and chased him home. I believe there was the very devil of a din, what with his yelps and the rattling of that tin on the road, and unhappily his homeward career was by the school from which my father and others were emerging after a parish meeting. Even disregarding the fact that that dog never troubled us again, I think the defence should have been allowed to put up a case.

Or take the more complicated matter of Tom Francis. My brother and I scaled the garden wall and helped ourselves to old Granny Francis's gooseberries. She did not see us but was informed of the theft by her young grandson, a boy of our age and a Methodist. After we had received due punishment, we decided to repay that treachery on the part of young Tom, so we waylaid him one morning when he was on his way to West Farm for milk. We made him take down his short trousers and then as a warning smeared the lower portions of his body with black mud from the handy Six-pits. For that we received the worst of all thrashings, and yet we had a good case. The quarrel was a private one between Tom and ourselves. Moreover, in acting on the information of informers, my father could have been shown that he was undermining the bases of our small society and putting a premium on treachery.

But there were escapades enough for which we received no punishment at all, except in the matter of conscience. Most notable was the matter of Wilson's plums. Wilson of the shop had his garden across the road, and in it were some fine fruit trees. Now my father happened to be out of the village one autumn night, so my brother and I took a risk and joined the horde of boys and youths on the Mound. Some one proposed a game of Hare and Hounds, and my brother and I were allowed to be the hares. We had made a circuit of the village and had arrived pantingly at Wilson's shop in the gathering dusk when my brother thought he heard the wheels of our cart, so we dodged into Wilson's garden and stood peering out through the low branches of a tree. But the cart wasn't our father's and then, as we straightened ourselves, something knocked against our heads. It was plums, egg plums, as we called them, huge in size, a golden yellow and dead ripe. We ate all we could and filled our pockets with the rest. Then at breakfast two mornings later my father had a dramatic announcement to make.

'Have you heard about Wilson's plums, mother? Some one went and stripped the whole tree!'

My mother was quite upset and asked what was being done about it.

'Potter think he know who did it,' my father told her. 'I shouldn't be surprised if he have his hands on 'em afore the day's out.'

I know that my face was scarlet and that I didn't dare look at my brother, but by some miracle neither of our parents happened to glance our way. I do know that we had a wretched day or two, for though the Potter of memory is heavy-footed, red-faced, wheezy and perspiring, he was to us the uncanny insight and the very terror of the law.

The mystery of the plums remained unsolved. Over twenty years later when my regiment was stationed near Dovercourt, I happened to hear that Wilson was living there, and I called on him, for he was a tradesman of the fine old school, who had been held in great respect. He was delighted to see me, and astounded when I told him the solution of that mystery of his plums. I also told him something that he had long forgotten, but which made him roar with laughter.

When there was no cake in the house—and there was rarely any after a Monday—we would be given biscuits for tea when my mother thought we deserved some small reward. A pennyworth would provide a few for each of us when we had eaten our bread and jam or bread and butter. You will note that there was never that unheard-of extravagance—bread and butter and jam.

The brand considered to give the best value for money was known as Thin Social. I knew the price well enough for I had been sent to buy them many times, but that afternoon I must have had a sense of my young importance as a customer. Wilson happened to be in the shop at the drapery counter.

'How much are Thin Social biscuits, Mr. Wilson?'

'Fourpence a pound,' he told me.

'A quarter of a pound, please,' I said importantly.

Wilson went on with what he was doing, remarking coolly to the girl at the other counter: 'Pennorth of Thin Social.'

Never in my life did I feel such a deflation of pride. But that afternoon in Dovercourt, Wilson told me a story I had never heard, and maybe because he was an older man than my father. It was about a son of old Tom, the weak-witted handyman who stole the carp. There was a question, it appeared, of sending this boy to some mental home, and a doctor from Ouseland was sent specially to examine him and report. This doctor's idea was to get the boy to talk and to

see if he could maintain any length of conversation. In order
to stimulate that talk he produced a penny, wagged it before
the boy's eyes, and then placed it on the table.

'Now then,' he said. 'What's that?'

'Heads!' said the boy promptly.

I have said that every individual member of our family had
his or her appointed tasks. Such a part of our lives did those
jobs become that there was no possible excuse that could
explain away forgetfulness or neglect. But if I had imagined
that when I went to Ouseland I should be relieved of at least
some of my tasks, I was to be very much mistaken. In fact
it was not long before it was discovered that I was having too
easy a time and before long I had to be up still earlier of mornings in order to complete the pre-breakfast duties, and when I
reached home on Saturday afternoons, off would come my
school clothes and on would go the oldest ones, and I might be
busy till night. My main task continued to be the cleaning of all
the yard and back premises, and a tidying of the front, though
there the removal of grass from between the stones was done
monthly. But in the early afternoon would be the collecting
of what we called baking things from the baker's. That use of
bakers' ovens on a Saturday for the whole of a week-end baking
was a system that saved the village much trouble and fuel, for as
soon as the bread was baked on a Saturday morning, along came
joints and pies for the oven, the cost being a halfpenny a dish.
But my mother disliked sending cakes and buns, which needed
a less mechanical baking. But the one thing I recall about
those Saturday jobs of mine was the occasion when, still in
my working clothes and incredibly dishevelled and dirty, I was
sent on some village errand, and with whom should I suddenly
come face to face than Old Benn on a bicycle. He had come
in from Ouseland to take tea at Heathley vicarage, and I still
recall my absolute horror at the sight of him and the deplorable
hand I made of lifting my cap.

In my holidays I mucked out sties, sheds, and stables: carted
dung and spread it; fed stock and took my share in all the
tasks of the field. I admit that I cared for few of them, and
most of all I hated loading hay or straw, for I was born with
a terror of heights and could never believe that my loading,
however quickly I drew in the hips, would save me from
collapse when we jolted off across a field and along the stony

6

lanes. In harvest I served a thatcher and soon came to lend
a hand with mowing. In fact I was a farmer in the making,
though I had had to pick up for myself the whys and where-
fores.

I shall never forget one early spring afternoon at Lammas
Meadows when I almost said good-bye to life. We had broken
in, as we thought, a young horse, and my brother—then about
fifteen—was deputed to take that horse to harrow a piece of
ground, and I accompanied him. The horse had little liking
for the job for perhaps he remembered the log that had been
allowed to swing against his legs to cure him of kicking, but
at any rate he suddenly halted, backed into the harrow and
then reared. We drew back as he kicked and plunged and
then we tried to free him in case he should do himself a
mischief. Then, and I do not know how, the chains came
free and one of them wrapped itself somehow round my leg,
and off set the horse at a gallop with me swishing at his heels.

I was dragged across that field and round it with my brother
hollering frantically for help. Each time I swung into the
horse's heels he lashed out at me, and each time the heels
miraculously went over my head. Then at last I fainted. When
I came to, there was my brother trying to revive me with a
bottle of ginger-beer he had run and fetched from the village.
The chain, it appeared, had at last come free of me by itself,
and I remember that at last we were able to catch the horse
and lead him home, though for some days I was shaky about
the legs.

But there were times when I had some leisure, though it
would generally be my mother who would beg it, and in that
I was far more fortunate than my contemporaries. Much of
that leisure would be spent on the heaths, and miles from the
village. On the Plains in spring I could hunt for peewits' eggs,
for one could see a keeper approaching across the flatness and
unless it were a shepherd one saw no other living soul. Except
perhaps John Pardon, for he played a game called golf, and
would bring a club there and some balls and indulge in a bit
of practice.

I loved best to go through Cranberry and on to Brackford
Heath, where there were pools in which one could bathe, or
wade as we called it. There would be stones to throw at the
innumerable rabbits, and pigeons to watch among the birches.
I could lie on a bed of pine-needles and read, or make myself

a bed of bracken. Once I brought home a brood of young wild ducks that I caught in a reach of a mere. Once I had the astounding sight of a swimming rabbit. Rabbits to us were good food, so when I saw that rabbit swimming across a narrow stretch of shallow water, I ran to head it off. At last I had it, but when I killed it and had a good look at it, it looked so repulsive with that sodden fur that the first time in my life I threw a rabbit away.

When Fox, who was a wheelwright and parish overseer, died at a ripe old age, his son Fred came back to the village to carry on the trade. He was a strange figure for our village; tall, and with a club foot, and with a monstrous head of hair that gave him the look of a poet or artist. And he was an artist in his way, for he combined with his carpentry the profession of photographer, and while the village still flourished, did a very good trade. Visitors would have their photographs taken, as would wedding-parties, and Fred also printed his own photographs of the village in post-card size. Many and many an hour did I spend at those prints, and as a reward for printing titles beneath some of the most important, I was often allowed to pose myself.

But the loveliest afternoons were those spent in his ancient carpenter's shop, which stood on a meadow just past the school in the Wortley Road. Its long windows were open to the road and through the broken panes would come the swallows who invariably built inside the shop itself. When they were feeding their young there would be scarcely a minute when there was not a bird.

In the corner of the shop would be timber, with seasoned pieces of special woods. There would be scores of tins of paint and a crate of glass, and tools like cramps too heavy for the bench. On the bench itself were the tools that had been used by generations of Foxes, and I remember specially the ancient chisels worn down almost to the shaft. Everywhere would be the sweet smell of sawn timber, mingling with the country scents that came through windows and door.

Fred was a superb tradesman, and as he worked I would watch him, and we would always talk. Forty years ago he made me some bookcases, or perhaps I should say cases for books, for they were what are now known as expanding bookcases, though then of my own invention and design. Each was two-foot-six in length, wide enough for the biggest book and of heights from six to twelve inches, and the largest sized had feet, since they would stand on a floor. They were of five-eights deal, and faced with oval splines, and backed with three-ply, and afterwards stained and varnished to resemble dark oak. The dove-tailings were perfect and to-day you can see never a joint that has sprung, though the cases have had much travelling.

Timber was cheap in those days. If one bought a salvaged load at Lynn after a shipwreck, then the price was incredibly small, but we rarely bought such loads since the salt was too hard on a plane. But I wonder if you could guess what those boxes cost me. Fred was satisfied with the price: indeed it was he who set it. The wood is as sound as a nut to this day, and, as I have said, the workmanship was of cabinet-making quality. And the average cost of each box, taking the deepest with the shallowest, was two shillings!

It is a mistaken idea that a humble villager is incapable of appreciating the best in literature and art. The walls of our cottages were not always covered with rubbish, and the wallpapers that women chose were often quiet and apt. I have seen Fred frame many pictures for cottagers, and though they were nearly always coloured supplements of papers and magazines, they were never devoid of some artistic value. As to books, I lent many to Fred, and it was always the best that he liked the most. I have lent books to many labouring men who have come to love Borrow and Hardy, and I have yet to meet such a man who did not love *The Bible in Spain*. Argue with me and disbelieve if you like, but I know that I am right. My own father became a voracious reader of the classics, with Hardy always his favourite. Once I lent *Pickwick Papers* to a village coachman. When I called at the cottage his wife said she hoped I was taking that book away, for her husband had neglected everything for it, and it was maddening to hear him in outbursts of laughter in which she was unable to join.

One brief pastime I remember which has its amusing side. What should come to Heathley one autumn night of fifty years ago but a circus!

I see now that it must have been the most insignificant tawdry affair that ever dared to call itself by such a name, but to us in the village it was an unheard-of excitement. All I remember of it is that the only performers were the proprietor and his wife, and that there was a small collection of wretched animals, including what was called a fat-tailed sheep and some kind of giant rat. I remember that when the woman was riding round on the back of the same fat pony that drew the smaller of the two vans, the man appeared as a clown. A joke that made us boys shriek with laughter was when he was unable to say, 'A bottle of port wine'. His version was, 'A bottle of pork rinds'.

But that circus incited me at least to imitation. There had been a dog that jumped through a hoop, and that was a shameful swindle, for on the small bills announcing the show had been a picture of the woman herself jumping through that hoop from the back of a resplendent steed. But as we had no dog suitable for such a trick, I proposed that we should do the act as shown on the bill. My partners were Tom Edwards and my third sister, who could run like a stag and was always in mischief. So a hoop was made and we adjourned to the scene of the performance.

This was Gaul's meadow, for on that meadow was his donkey and an orchard hid the meadow from the farm-house. But the trouble was that the donkey refused to co-operate. When I, in my capacity of ring-master, touched him up, as we called it, with my father's best whip that had been abstracted for the occasion, he made no movement at all but went unconcernedly on with his grazing. So my sister straddled him and forthwith he came to life. Up went his hind legs and my sister was sprawling. Then Tom tried and met the same fate. With something of my father's impatience I told Tom to hold the whip, and I mounted the old donkey. Maybe he knew I was the head of the concern for he actually took a step or two before hurling me into the air. The fall knocked me out for a minute and when I blinked and sat up, I was alone. The others had taken to their heels, and coming towards me was old Ben Gaul. I grabbed the whip and departed too.

Only a few years later, at the turn of the century, there was a stir throughout all Breckland when Barnum and Bailey's Circus came to Bury St. Edmunds. Special excursions were run, and many, including my father, went from our village. I was at school and unable to go, but we children heard of the wonders from my father. I remember he looked at me and with a twinkle in his eye remarked that it was a pity there was now no donkey in the village since Ben Gaul had gone. That was the first time I knew he had been aware of our afternoon's escapade.

It was at about that time, so my sisters have since told me, that I began the telling of stories. I doubt if I composed them. It was far more likely that they were gathered from my general reading, though my sisters have insisted that they were not. But I do remember starting a novel, and that when I was twelve. All I know is that it was about Cavaliers and Round-heads, and the scene opened in the Wortley Road. I think I wrote a hundred foolscap pages and, to show the queer tricks that memory plays, though I can remember no word that I wrote I can see the very paper and the thin ink of my very writing, and I can feel the fragrant cool of a summer afternoon through the bedroom window where I would make much of a mystery by shutting myself in.

It was not so long after that, that my travels across the heaths took me as far as Topleigh village, and the church. That church made a tremendous impression on me, with its paintings on the walls and the high, pen-like pews of its ancient notabilities. In fact I wrote an article on that church and, thinking it was good, submitted it to John Balfour. He insisted that it should be sent to the *Norfolk News,* and in its subsidiary *The Ouseland and Hareborough Times* it duly appeared. My mother still has it, but I have not dared to read it. All I know is that its style was modelled on Sir John Lubbock's *Pleasures of Life,* which I had received in the last year of the Queen's reign as a German prize, and that I had some difficulty in embellishing my effort with suitable quotation. It was years before I learned to appraise such things as the pretty-pretty of Lubbock and the forced explosiveness of Carlyle, and to learn that always in my hands had been the Bible and Bunyan. Abana and Pharpar are always better than the waters of Israel. 'If the prophet had bid thee do some great thing, wouldst thou not have done it? How much rather then when he saith to thee, Wash and be clean.'

Perhaps the greatest day of the year for us children was not Christmas Day but Boxing Day, for it was then that we gave a small party that included grown-ups. The routine of that day never varied, for my father would always contrive to have somewhere to spend the day at rabbiting, and with us would always go John Till the shoemaker, son of Josh Till. Let those shoot pheasants from stands who have the taste for such a shooting-gallery kind of sport, but give me a day's tramping with a gun or a day after rabbits. To a boy such a day was a succession of thrills. There would first be the beating of gorse—away out at Illboro or Snettley it might be—when the dogs had a chance of running down a rabbit. Then would come the placing of purse nets over the holes of the big burrows and the putting in of cooped ferrets, and the desperate excitement of waiting for a bolt. Then when the cooped ferrets were caught there would be the line ferret; the digging down to where, five feet below the ground maybe, one had heard the ferret at work, and then when ferret and rabbit were brought out, the further excitement of finding another rabbit or two at the end of that same cul-de-sac.

Then as the youngest member of the party I would have to make a fire, and a roasting one it would be, with us sitting by it at our meal in the lee of a hedge. And so till we jogged home in the pony-cart with our catch, and I remember that when I had changed my clothes and was sitting by the fire awaiting tea, I would be half asleep from the keen healthy air of that day on some open heath or breck.

John Till would always come to tea that night, and I can still see our vast and festive board for that stupendous meal. Afterwards there would be nuts and oranges and finally a supper of cakes and cocoa for us and the guests. How my mother managed to provide it I do not know. Maybe that is something else that must be placed to the credit of the imponderables.

In John Till's shop I spent many a pleasant hour, for if one were sent there on an errand, it was hard work to get away. John has been dead for some years now, but I can still see him in his leather apron crouching over his work, and mark the deft play of his fingers as he made wax-ends or sewed a sole or took one by one the brads from his mouth to tap unerringly into a heel. In the corner of the shop would be the pickling tin with its leather, and there would be heaps of ancient lasts from which the village boots for generations had been made. Once he showed me one that had been used for my grandfather, but that age of village-made boots had gone. Our boots of fifty years ago had begun to come from Walter Addis's shop and at a price enormously below the cost of John's fashioning, though whether cheapness in that instance was cheapness indeed, I have my serious doubts.

Of my mother's discipline I have not spoken, for so un-obstrusive was it that I remember very little of it. I do know it tended more to a rule of love than of fear, and that it was effective. But it was with what I might call morals that my mother concerned herself. My father never mentioned right and wrong; all he did was punish summarily what he considered a commission of the latter and neglect of the former. My mother would be at pains to point out *why* this was wrong and that was right. From her I learned a terror of bankruptcy when a neighbour so failed, and the sure end of those extravagant enough to eat bread and butter with cold meat. We shared her dislike of dancing and we knew all the implications of the arrival of Catholics in the village with the coming of Mrs. Green and French maids. In the matter of religion my mother was indeed something of a martinet. To question a word of Holy Writ was a heinous offence, and I remember an occasion when she made no protest against my receiving a severe thrashing. It was after a morning of Sunday school. Walter Addis had taken us boys as usual and we had been reading the ancient Bible stories as we did year in and out, and he had questioned us afterwards.

'Why did Moses go up alone to the mountain?' he asked me.

Now all my life I have been pestered by a devil of perversity who makes me do the most inexplicable and preposterous things; the same devil, for instance, who even to-day will whisper just before a bowler delivers a ball that I must run up the pitch and smite it. That devil was at my ear that morning.

'To do his jobs,' I said, and the phrase is a Breckland euphemism for relieving nature. Maybe I had in mind that other euphemism of Saul's going aside into a cave to 'cover his feet', but there the answer was and somehow it was reported to my father.

But about that discipline of my mother I still hold, however indignantly she may deny it, that a grandparent will treat with more latitude and have for grandchildren a deeper inward affection than for children of that same age. I wonder what would have been my reward if I had shown an ignorance of Holy Writ such as was demonstrated by one of my young nephews even at the age of six. He and Tony Procter, of the same age, were going up to bed at my house when Peter observed for the first time a picture of the infant Samuel on the landing wall, and their grandmother overheard the following brief conversation.

'Who's that?' demanded Peter.

'Samuel,' said Tony.

'Who's Samuel?'

Tony said it was Samuel, and that was that.

'Well, where'd he have it took?' asked Peter.

I wonder, too, what would have happened to a young sister and myself if we had engaged in only the opening words of an argument that took place on the lawn beneath the open window of the breakfast-room where my mother was sitting. The speakers were Tony and his sister Joan, then aged seven. She was the most delightful of children, but at times inclined to be the least bit pious. The conversation was related by my mother to my eldest sister, who first repeated it to me. I set it down in dramatic form.

J. Tony, God is wonderful. He can do anything in the world.

T. (After some pondering). Oh, no, He can't.

J. Tony, you wicked boy! If your granny heard that she'd be ever so angry. God *can* do anything.

T. He can't.

J. What can't He do then?

T. He can't make a cake as big as the house.

J. Oh, He can.

T. He can't.

J. He can!

(Several can'ts and cans, terminated by a suggestion from Joan herself that she should ask God about it.)

T. All right. You ask Him.

J. So I will then.

(Hands were forthwith clasped, eyes meekly closed and face uplifted.)

God, can you make a cake as big as the house?

(The treble changed to a squeak in which came the heavenly verdict.)

Yes, I can.

T. It wasn't God who said that, it was you!

J. It wasn't. It was God.

T. It wasn't.

J. It was!

(Several more wasn'ts and was's and then a suggestion from Joan that Tony should make his own inquiries. So his hands were clasped and face uplifted.

T. God, can you make a cake as big as the house?
(His curiously gruff voice changed to a squeak, and again came a reply.)
No, I can't.
J. Oh, you wicked boy! It wasn't God who said that, it was you!
T. It wasn't. It was God.
J. It wasn't.
T. It was!

And there, I regret, that the argument ended, for at last their Granny intervened.

Chapter VII

A VILLAGE ROAD

THAT one should write a chapter on a village road, even with no straining of material, may seem a strange and even unnecessary thing, especially when I say that those two miles and more of road had on them no houses whatever. But to me that road was always, and still is, the loveliest in the world. I calculate that in my schooldays I walked its length more than two thousand times. I knew almost each twig and blade of grass and frond of bracken. It was the road I first saw when I came on a peaceful summer evening in the pony-cart with my father from Fenwold to my old and yet new home. It was the road I took when I went out into the world. It was the road I saw in the eye of the mind when in the lonely places of the world I thought of home. It was the road by which one left, but it was also the road by which one always came back.

I would like you to bear with me while I draw you a picture of that road, so that you, too, may see it in the eye of the mind. We knew it as the Wortley Road, and it began just past the school, Fred Fox's shop, and the gates of Home Meadow where a side road led to church and Hall. From that moment it became like the aisle of some immense cathedral, for even the hedges of the meadow to the right were set close with oaks and elms, and they interlaced to form a vast arch with the trees of the woods, and that great avenue continued till the Bambridge drift.

In the woods on the left before the private road to the Hall stood the keepers' cottages, the nearer of which was Field's, and when one passed that way at night there would be immediate barking of the black retrievers whose kennels lay beside the path. But only at the private road were the cottages visible, and except distantly across the meadows to the right

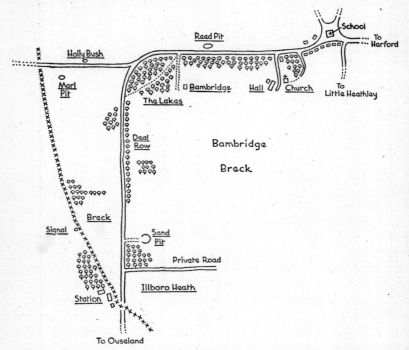

there was never the sign of house or cottage till Wortley Station was reached

Past the Bambridge track, at the end of which was a keeper's cottage, the road swung left to encircle the large wood known as The Lakes, through which ran a private path. The fork to the right went on past Gallow's Hill, across the Peddar's Way to the heath country of Tottley. Just along it stood a monstrous holly bush from which to Heathley school was said to be a measured mile. A great uncle of mine, Joseph Aldgate by name, was said to have frequently betted that he would run it in his ordinary clothes in under five minutes, and never to have lost a bet.

Two things happened where The Lakes ended: the Deal

Row began and so did a granite road. Up till then the road had been rough, for the method of metalling was to strew its whole surface with white marl from the Marl Pit, and then to cover that with cracked flints. There was no steam-roller to roll in those flints, which relied for their binding on the ordinary traffic, and though they would be scattered in the autumn, some would lie loose all summer, and all drivers of horses carried a knife with that special tool for extracting stones from the horses' hooves.

That long line of ancient deal trees was a notable sight, even if the Great Gale had made a few gaps, and their reddish trunks would glow a vivid orange-scarlet in an evening sun. Through them one saw the great stretch of the breck, most of which, save for poor crops of lucerne, had fallen out of cultivation. To the right were also poor fields, that still managed to produce thin crops of rye. That side of the road was bordered by a thick hedge of spruce and ran till the Heathley boundary ended at a point just opposite the new private road to Little Heathley. There one stood at the top of the hill with the station lying below, but the best use of that hill vantage-point was for a glance at the signal away in the distance, for if it were down, then one would have to hurry to catch the train. From that hill, too, one could see across the valley to the other far signal on the Wortley side, and know if a train were approaching from Ouseland.

And that in brief is the Wortley Road, lovely throughout its length and as lovely in its vistas across the lonely country side. Blackberries topped its hedges and among them grew honeysuckle so that with the first dews of evening the air was heavy with scent. Bracken sprawled along the verges. Rabbits were everywhere among their burrows on the brecks, and where there were chance stacks would be the aloof indifferent pheasants.

The train I took for school was the first of the day and known as the quarter past nine, and when it roared out of the cutting through the woods by the far signal its sound would reach Heathley and men could check their watches. My time for leaving home was at half-past eight, which allowed three-quarters of an hour for the two and a quarter miles. By daylight I was indifferent as to rides, and for the first mile at least my head would be in a book as I tried to learn the homework that had been neglected the previous night. If it were winter I would make my quickest way to the station and never in the whole of those five years did I miss the train. The station-master—Urrey, I think was his name—used to lend me books, and as he had an extensive collection of those by Mrs. Henry Wood and Miss Braddon, I would take them for my mother too.

But in spring and early summer that journey was far more than a mere reaching of a railway station, and I would scheme to leave home as early as I could. There would be, for instance, a periodical inspection of the Reed Pit to see how water-hens' nests were progressing, and I would be on the look-out for that little floating island of mud beneath which might be buried a didapper's eggs. Next I would take that private path through The Lakes, and always with an eye and ear for a keeper. That short cut was an illusory one for the path twisted and turned to avoid the trees blown down by the gale, and I think I took it only because it made the journey different.

As soon as the spruce hedge was reached I would take its far side where, hidden from the road, I would beat it with a stick as I proceeded. This was to disturb nesting blackbirds or thrushes, and make them disclose their nests. If I found a new egg I would pierce it and suck it, or I would mark down the nest for a future visit. To blackbirds I was particularly hostile, like my father, for we always shot for the pot or pocket, and it is infuriating to be in reach of a rabbit or hare and then to have the game disturbed by a squawking black-bird, as was often the case.

But in my pocket would be three or four good stones that I had picked up farther back along the road, and these would be thrown at any chance rabbit. Practice made most village boys deadly at stone-throwing. To miss a sitting rabbit at ten yards was almost unthinkable, and why we never got more of them was because they were too alert and wary to sit. There was a time when, given three stones, I would bet that standing at one telegraph post I would hit the next, and if you think that is easy, then you might try it for yourself. The one shot that I do remember was at a roosting pheasant at a range of some ten yards, and I hit it in the head so that it fell like the stone itself. But that was in the wood approaching the Hall and I was scared to pick it up for fear of keepers. When I reached home I told my father, and he at once went in search of it. Maybe I had only stunned it, but at any rate it had gone.

Just before the spruce hedge ended I would leave it, for maybe in the distance I could hear the train as it roared across the heaths by the Top Breck. Or, as each side of the hill was never without a rabbit, I might have time for another shot or two, though at too great a range ever to bring success. Generally, too, at the top of the hill I would be overtaken by a trap from the Lion, or the Vicarage or the Hall, bringing passengers for the same train. If I heard a friendly call and my name, that would be Miss Maud Pardon cycling to the station, for at Ouseland she was for a time having lessons on the organ from one of the school's music-masters.

As for the homeward journey when the nights were light, their pace would depend on what lay at the other end. If I knew that there would be cricket practice on the Park, for instance, I would fly home, eat the hot meal my mother would always have for me, promise to be back in time to complete my homework, and then disappear from the house. But I remember one evening when I came through The Lakes and what should I see sitting on a bough of a fallen oak but two young owls. When my hand went out they spat at me, and that gave me pause. But by a dexterous use of the emptied satchel and my handkerchief I secured them both, and my father made a special hutch for them. Then one night they disappeared, though the netting of the hutch was intact. We were given to believe that they were stolen, but I think my father had let them go, for the stench from their diet had brought complaints from my mother.

But that long road on dark winter nights was a different place. When I first had to take it my mother was frightened for me, but I can honestly say that I never felt the least fear. Pitch black as the nights might be, and heavy with rain or sleet, one could still faintly discern the road. My mother would tell me to sing to keep my courage up, and my father would advise that if I met a tramp or suspicious character, I was to call as if he himself were only just behind, and then take to my heels. But I had my own methods, which were to shorten the journey by trotting till I was out of breath and then walking till I was ready to trot again.

To a nervous boy that Wortley Road on a dark night must have been a fearsome place. The trees that had given shade in summer now made shadows as dark as hell's mouth, and though I was never really frightened, I was always glad to get past the fork and on the homeward stretch, for that narrow part by The Lakes always brought to my mind the Valley of the Shadow and the fiends and goblins that daunted Christian before his fight with Apollyon. It was past that lonely spot that I would always trot at my hardest, and then when I had mounted the slight rise to the Bambridge track, across the fields I might perhaps discern the friendly lights of Puddledock.

Always on those dark nights I would be listening for the sound of a cart behind me, and the hope of a ride, and I would always be glancing back for the friendly gleam of cart-lamps. Perhaps my rides averaged twice a week, and it did not matter to me whose cart or trap it was. Sam Smith's coal-cart was just as much a ride and company as was a rare trap or wagonette from Vicarage or Hall. And I cannot tell you with what incredible longing I awaited the coming of Valentine's Day, when the time of labourers changed from winter hours to from six to six. It was never light then at six, but at least it was dusk, and I would get well on my way before darkness really fell. Even more than for Christmas, and though that was my birthday, I would long for the coming of Valentine's and the end of that lonely winter walk.

Friday night was the one night of the week when I was sure of a ride, for that was when William Cash came to Wortley station for our weekly papers. I would wait by the old black pony till he had collected the huge bundle, and then he would get in the low cart and turn the pony round. By that time the crossing gates would be open and there would be the sound of the train puffing its way towards the heaths. Up the hill the pony would walk with the flickering lamps illuminating no more maybe than its ears, and then at the top the reins would be shaken and the homeward journey would have begun.

I cannot rightly say how much I owe to those homeward journeys with William Cash, but it is much. He was widely if indiscriminately read, and a Radical who digested each scrap of political report and gossip, and on those rides it would be politics that he chiefly talked, with the talk ranging from the Deceased Wife's Sister's Bill, it might be, to the latest capers of the Irish Members. He was a pro-Boer as we called it, and tried to instil into me a hatred of capitalism, and of South African capitalists in particular. A curious irony that he himself should have come in later years to boast of his invested monies, and that I should have met on his own superb cricket ground at Old Buckenham, Lionel Robinson, whose name I had heard Cash mention twenty years before.

Joe Chamberlain was the object of his most intense hatreds as one who had renounced Radicalism for capitalist and Unionist flesh-pots. I came to hate Joe Chamberlain too, and from the frequent sight of him in those *Westminster Gazette* cartoons, could draw my own caricature of him with my eyes shut. I admit I could also do the same of Kruger. But what vital and intensely personal things were politics in those far-off days! When we hated, we hated, and when we cheered for our side it was with a fervour and intensity that came from some-thing deeper than we knew. It was with the passing of the Irish Members that much vitality left Parliament, and with the coming of Labour and the decline of the Liberal Party, politics were never quite the thing they had been. Cash loved those Irish Members. I can still see his curl of the lip and his dry chuckle as he told me one night of the remark of Tim Healy, I think it was, in the House. The Secretary for War had assured the House—and that was at the time of accumulated disasters—that every available horse had been sent to South Africa.

'And all the asses,' broke in Tim.

But one thing I do know. William Cash in his own often petty and unscrupulous way, was to become a bitter enemy of mine, and yet at this moment I know I would give much to be back at one of those nights again, the old pony jogging toward home and the dry, sarcastic voice of William Cash in my young ears, with its talk of politics that *were* politics or village history that was in a way my history.

But those rides were to have a sudden end, and for an extra-ordinary reason. The whole affair was a local sensation and even the Norwich papers were at last sufficiently impressed to take note of it. It was always known as the affair of the Parish Pump, and as such is still well remembered.

In order to celebrate the coronation of Edward the Seventh, the village collected—irrespective of what was needed for a dinner and sports—the large sum of over a hundred pounds. Then the village was divided on the question of how the money was to be spent. I have actually forgotten what my

side wanted—and when I say that I mean my father's side
and that of Peacock, the third of a triumvirate of Heathley
Radicals—but I know that Cash's party carried the day, and
the digging for the village pump which they favoured was at
once commenced. I believe there was a dowser and water
was reported where it was wanted, which was at a corner of
the Mound.

For weeks the drilling apparatus was there, and, since I am
a dowser myself, I have often wondered why water was not
struck. But struck it never was. On went the drilling and
with always the promise that water was on the point of
spouting, and then came the time when the monies were
expended and it was actually proposed that a rate should be
levied for further drilling. Fox, as I have said, was the then
rate-collector, and other members of the Cash party were
Sutton, head gardener at the Hall, and Eli Shaw, Squire
Finch's coachman. But you may guess the fury of our faction
at that proposal to tax us to try to make good the other
faction's mistakes.

And that was where I entered the scene. Long years of
sitting at the feet of my father, and Peacock and William Cash,
had made of me as fervent a factionist as any, and I had been
filled with fury at the thought of that parish rate. Now at
Ouseland we had been reading Macaulay's poems, including
the *Armada*. Suddenly an idea came to me, and that lunch-
time and on the way home in the train I began to write.

Mine was what might be called a parody with a purpose, and
as such had no literary merit, but it did succeed in hitting a
nail or two on the head. I would call it now the showily
clever work of a schoolboy with an ear for metre and rhyme,
and far too anxious for the success of the latter to make sure of
all his facts. And some of it was not too courteous, to say the
least of it.

Attend all ye who list to hear our famous Heathley's praise.
I sing of the thrice famous deeds she wrought in recent days.

That was the imitative beginning. As for some of the more
scandalous lines, I instance:

Ned and Tom and Leonard John, and Sutton—oft called Tad,[1]
And Fox the old, the treasurer bold, who wisdom never had.

[1] Turd.

and, most devastating of all, a reference to William Cash, who had been a tailor and whose nickname was Bradford Billy.

Of Bradford he supposed to be, and famous for his stitches

But I quote no more, for to do so would be to you as unprofitable as trying to follow without notes the allusions in the *Dunciad*. But the last lines were these:

Our cash to spend they now intend to open Fox's coffers
And to reject, not to inspect, all wise and prudent offers.
But what say you, parishioners? Is this thing to be borne?
Your money to be wasted? Your trust held up to scorn?
If not, show your intentions. Put the Pump where it should go,
Set up your backs against the tax, and down with Shaw and Co.!

Now I did not want my name connected with that effusion, so when I had shown it to Peacock, I intended to show it also to my father perhaps and then to burn it. But Peacock saw possibilities. At his suggestion I printed it in large letters on the back of some wallpaper. I put no signature to it and he then came by night, as it were, to the Reading Room and pasted it on a wall. When the village youths and young men assembled there, you can imagine the sensation. Endless copies were made and soon the whole village was either roaring with laughter or furious with rage. Though I would never acknowledge authorship the village attributed that poem to me, and, now I come to think of it, I can think of no one else to whom it might have been attributed.

But that next Friday night there was no ride for me in Cash's cart. Eternal vigilance may be the price of freedom, but I paid dear for my first defence. But politics as I said, even of the parochial kind, were taken seriously, though I still think that a man with a geniality of soul and a saving humour might have taken that squib and me—and himself—less seriously. I do know that when on a summer night Cash passed me in his cart, I felt a peculiar sort of shame, and not all of it was for myself. I should add that from the enemy there came only one retort to our squib—a piece of wretched doggerel said to have been written by Cash's daughter, a school teacher. All I remember of it is that it sneered at me as a charity scholar: one whose education was paid for by the rates!

But, as I said, the affair was reported in the Norwich papers and caused much stir. And the fact remains that no parish rate for Pump purposes was ever levied. All that happened was that Heathley lost its money and had nothing to show for it but a certain disfigurement of its Mound. My mother has recently told me that Peacock, now a magistrate and an honoured one, still has a copy of that poem. If these words should meet his eyes, I hope he will send me a copy, for it is well over fifty years since I saw it.

For five years I walked the Wortley Road. For five years I went backwards and forwards by that little local train, and in all that time there were only two occasions when the routine of walk and train, train and walk was broken. But there is an exaggeration, for on the most celebrated occasions there was still a train to follow the walk. That was on a never-to-be-forgotten morning when—incredible as if the sun had turned to a moon—the train did not come roaring across the heaths at a quarter past nine. I sat in the station that fine summer morning and waited and waited, and at last word came that the train had broken down. I believe it was almost midday when it arrived, and morning school was virtually over when I walked into the schoolroom. I heard afterwards from one of the boarders that Old Benn had remarked that he knew at once that the fault of the late arrival was not mine, so complacent had been the look of my young face.

Then on a certain Saturday Old Benn was in one of his obstinate moods and kept the train boys late. I ran all the way to the Ouseland Station and was just in time to see my train draw out. But occasionally it halted a couple of hundred yards on because of the Bury train, so I continued my run along the platform and the line, with porters yelling to me to come back. But the train did not halt that morning, so I went on my way along the line. At Rudgham I skirted the station and then went back to the line again, and so to Wortley home.

The only other time that I walked the eight miles across the heaths from Ouseland was when I was commissioned by my father to call at a certain house in Ouseland and collect a puppy, and that puppy I carried home from Ouseland in my arms. She was rather more than a puppy, for I remember that that same night my father began her training. That was Nell, the most celebrated bitch that ever worked in Breckland, but of her we may hear more later.

Postscript.

Since the above chapter was written I paid, after many years, a short visit to Heathley. It was in August of last year and I was on my way to Tinkersham from Ouseland where I had stayed the night at the Bell. The tales that had been told me of the desecration of the Wortley Road seemed too incredible for belief and I knew I had to see that road again for myself.

But what I saw was more than a desecration. It was as if my youth had been buried and the grave itself befouled. Only a few days before, the ancient trees of the Deal Row had been wantonly felled and their ghastly stumps still showed a pallid white. All that first mile from Wortley station was now merely a lane between monstrous plantations of spruce. Had there been here and there a clump or two of deciduous trees there might still have been a vista of the once lovely brecks, but all the earth was densely covered with that monotonous obscurity of regimented fir, and through that dark lane I fled so quickly in my car that it was never the nightmare it might since have been had I lingered.

Chapter VIII

HEAD OF THE HOUSE

PERHAPS I can see my father best in myself, though I have inherited most of his faults and few of his virtues—except perhaps three. Like him I am never so happy as when at work. I have a zest for life and I know that a multiplicity of interests is more exciting, even if less profitable, than an absorption in one. There are times when I find myself using his very words and phrases, and in broad Norfolk, and employing his very gestures. I am awake to his ironies and outspoken to my own short-term detriment, though occasionally long-term profit. Poaching is still in my blood though it is many a year since I indulged in it, and I am a disfranchised man now Radicals have ceased to exist.

In giving an only too truthful account of that trip to Yarmouth I may have seemed somewhat unjust, or to have accentuated the minor faults. But it is true that he was a man of infinite moods, just as he was many-sided in interests and activities. His active brain was as restless as his hands. Dawn saw him rise and only night saw him cease, and when he worked it was with a remorseless, irresistible energy. And a strong personality outspoken in his views, obstinate in opinion, intolerant of both injustice and delay, must necessarily have trodden on many toes. I recall a piece of advice he once gave me. 'Don't let people tread on your toes,' he said. 'Don't even let them get near enough to look like treading.' And when his case was just, he feared no man, whatever his status and possessions.

I have indicated none too clearly that he was bilingual. Norfolk came more trippingly to his tongue, as once it did to mine, but when it so pleased him he could speak an English better than my own, for it was garnished with sinewy words and homely metaphor such as Bunyan never despised. Though his arguments generally lacked logic and sequence, yet his manner was convincing and he had the sure knack of holding a listener. Short and tremendously strong, he carried himself so that he looked inches taller than his height, and that was how it was with his arguing. But when he spoke of local history and customs, there was no illogic, and it was then that he could have held no matter what listener.

I recall an occasion which had an unexpected sequel. I should be about nine years old at the time, and he had purchased some rabbits at West Farm. On a fine November morning I was with him when he was rabbiting near the Holly Bush, and all at once we were joined by a stranger. I forget his name. For weeks I have been trying to remember it, but I know it was a famous name. Its owner, an elderly man, was staying at the Hall but having no taste for sport had left the shooting-party and had taken the walk that brought him our way. He must have been of an inquiring mind, for aristocrat though he obviously was, he soon got into conversation with my father.

My father told him the history of the fields where we were at work, and how they had fallen into disuse once they had ceased to be marled from the Marl Pit. He also gave a history of the Hall where he was staying. What else they talked about I cannot remember, but I know that the old gentleman stayed while we were having our meal in the lee of a hedge and all the time the two were talking. Then he looked at his watch in dismay and said he would be late for lunch. My father said he could get to the Hall in a quarter of an hour.

'Perhaps if my legs were as long as yours, my friend,' the old gentleman said.

'So they are, sir,' my father told him. 'You and I are the same build. That hat of yours mightn't fit me, but that coat would.'

A day or two later a parcel was delivered at our house. It was that overcoat, a gift from the old gentleman himself. I can still see its fine cut and the handsome black velvet collar, and I know my father would wear it only on great occasions.

I believe, too, that the coat was given as an appreciation of an engrossing morning, and not because of what had never really existed—an implication of request.

Take the tales that he would tell us when we were children. We had heard them innumerable times and yet they always sounded fresh and astonishing. There was the story of how as a young man in London he had been promoted to some sort of responsible post at a large spice mill, and how one day the lower storeys of that mill caught fire. When my father was aware of it the flames were all about him, and he had to jump for life. His shirt-sleeves were still rolled up and all he did was to close his eyes and leap. When he came to himself he was in hospital. But for the fact that he was a teetotaler, so the doctor had said, he would never have survived. On his arms as he rolled back his coat-sleeves to show us, were the scars of terrible burns.

When he came to that moment of the leap into space, we children would hold our breath, as if the years might mysteriously have changed the outcome. And there was the story of how unknowingly he had carried a quarter of a ton on his back. I know that story to be true, for when Wortley Hall was rebuilding, there was a foreman of navvies there who would make a bet to carry five sacks of cement, and he was a man of less concentrated strength than my father. How he would do it would be to take two sacks under each of his arms and have a fifth laid across his shoulders, and with that load he would totter the length of a workshop for a gallon of beer.

Above all we children loved the various tales of a man known to us as Corporal. He seemed to have been the Till Eulenspiegel of that spice mill, and the tears would run down my father's cheeks when he related some hilarious exploit. So real a person was this Corporal to myself that often when I saw some one approaching in the distance, I would wonder if by chance it might be Corporal. And as for those tales in general, there was more to their holding power than the credulity of a child and interest inherent in a tale itself. For as my father spoke, he always saw. He was the eye-witness even of himself, and his face would glow and his hands quiver with the intensity of those things that he saw again with his inward eye.

I remember a certain Tory—and a Methodist at that—whom my father was determined politically to convert, and that was old George Blanche who was steward for a time at Little Heathley. One evening my father tackled him and the argument got round to the suffragettes, and to them my father was violently opposed. George was a stolid listener who would let a speaker run on, and only if driven to it would he express an opinion of his own. But that evening—and my father would tell the story against himself—George was even more stolid than usual, and perhaps because my father was even more vehement and long-winded, Finally, at the very end, when no more arguments presented themselves, my father asked for a verdict, and George was to make his sole contribution.

'Am I right or am I not?' my father demanded.

'Whuh, yes,' said George whose wits had long lost track of argument. 'I agree wi' you, neighbour. If they want the woot[1] let 'em ha' the woot.'

One test of the genuineness of a man's political opinions is the point at which he refuses all compromise. Even if it was usually only in spirit that my father had to be a village Hampden there were three instances to my knowledge in which he stood up fearlessly for village rights. One has been related elsewhere concerning a right of way that was closed by Squire Finch. The second was of much the same kind, though I am less certain of the details.

I know it involved the price fixed for sand from a pit in The Lakes. Squire Finch maintained that the pit was wholly a private one and a prevailing price could be charged. My father disagreed. He had heard from his father that the parish had been concerned with making the track to that pit and that in consequence a special price had been laid down. How many generations had passed since that agreement was made I cannot say, but Finch was sufficiently impressed to consult certain documents found among the deeds, and then he sent for my father and told him he had been right. Then he handed him a paper. It said that from then on he was to have for his personal use and GRATIS—Finch himself printed the word like that— all the sand he might at any time require from that sand pit. I quote that instance as a tribute to the character of two men, and not least to that of Finch who so generously acknowledged himself in the wrong.

As a footnote I can state from personal knowledge that

[1] Vote.

when the old squire died it so happened that my father was in need of sand from that pit. As a matter of courtesy he informed the agent of his intention of drawing it out. Unhappily the precious paper could not be found, but the agent refused to accept his word or that of myself as witness. I can still see him leaning back in his chair and blandly informing us that in any case since the original benefactor was dead, the paper would then be of no effect.

The other question of a right of way was between my father and the Reverend and happened when I was quite young. John Pardon sent for him.

'I'm informed,' he said, 'that you have been taking a short cut through my kitchen garden and that you've made a gap in one of the hedges. I can't understand why.'

My father explained. Along a vicarage hedge was a right of way and for some reason that path had been blocked. My father had therefore turned into the garden and had then emerged behind the obstruction. That had admittedly seemed pretty high-handed, and the Reverend was quick to point it out.

'You look it up in one of your law books, sir,' my father told him. 'The law entitle me to take the nearest way no matter whose property I have to go on.'

The Reverend looked it up and found the statement sufficiently correct. The obstruction was immediately removed and no more was said.

As a class my father hated squires and parsons, and though I never knew a squire he did more than tolerate, yet I knew individual parsons for whom he had a profound respect and even a very strong liking. John Pardon was one, and at least a couple of Illboro parsons were others.

There was no work which my father despised and I am of his opinion, even if 'the dignity of labour' may be to some very much of a catch phrase. With a growing family to support and the fact that he was both Radical and Ranter against him, my father would undertake any work within his power and capabilities. For old Parson Bird—dead and gone these fifty years and more—he was a kind of estate carpenter, builder, and decorator, and he was even occasionally consulted over the old man's sermons, for Bird was something of an eccentric. Many a happy day have I spent in that lonely vicarage, hidden among the trees. Illboro itself was so small and remote a hamlet that it was the only one to my recollection that did not contrive somehow at some time in its history to raise a cricket team.

The first vicar—or was it rector?—of Illboro that I knew was Bird's successor, and that would be when I was about ten years old. Bird must have recommended my father to him, for the work went on as it had done for years and by that I mean that my father would so scheme that when no work was available nearer home, he would go at once to Illboro and get on with something deliberately left unfinished. B.—I dare allude to him no more closely than that—was as far removed from his predecessor as could be. I think he must have been about thirty-five when I first saw him. He was superbly proportioned as befitted a middle-of-the-boat Cambridge blue, and his manner was free and easy. It was said that his wife kept the purse-strings tightly drawn, and I know that often before he could make his morning visit to Wortley Stone Brig —the inn in the dip past Wortley Station—he would borrow a shilling from my father.

'Give me a shilling, Home,' he would say. 'The old lady's a bit close this morning.'

It was she who paid the bills and commissioned new jobs. For her my father designed and made what must have been the finest fowl-houses ever seen in Breckland, for he was a man of remarkably inventive mind. Years afterwards he showed me a catalogue from a very famous firm to whom he had sub-mitted—at Mrs. B.'s suggestion—a drawing of one of those houses. The firm had replied that they were interested but at that moment not in a position to go further into the matter. In that catalogue, however, were fowl-houses embodying my father's very inventions and hailing them as the very latest thing. I advised against taking the matter up, for the B.'s had left Illboro and there was no real evidence.

B. was very much of a hero to me, and he and my father got on like two bugs in a rug. I think it appealed to my father's keen sense of irony that the monies that B. borrowed were always added to a bill. And he and B. would yarn together by the hour. One story my father would relate in suitable com-pany and which I risk in this, is the account of why B. was sent down—if sent down he was.

B. said there was a party one glorious summer night on the lawn of some don's house, and that lawn sloped down to the river. B. and the rest of the conspirators bought up every chamber-pot in Cambridge and the district and just after dusk filled them with combustibles and set them afloat. I can see my father telling that tale, eyes twinkling and the laughing wrinkles at the corners of his eyes.

'Can't you see them old gotches,'[1] he would say. 'First one come sailin' past and then another, and them gentlemen on the lawn tryin' to knock them over with oars and what not. And them ladies all horrified and scutterin' into the house with their faces all red.'

Most of Heathley managed to live and yet the financial stability—particularly in the case of tenant farmers—was balanced on a razor edge. There were never spare margins, and swings had always somehow to compensate for round-abouts. Pigs were always gold or dirt, and somehow my father rarely had the luck to buy in the cheapest market and sell in the dearest. Like others he had to have his corn threshed at the first available moment. He could never hold for a possible rise in price, for corn had to pay rent and the accumulation of bills.

But there were special peculiarities about the economics of the Home family. You may have been wondering how it was that a man who had so many activities and who worked such long hours should not have been free from all financial worry. The answer lies in many things, and chiefly in my father himself.

First of all there was much competition for work. Heathley had that London builder, and there was a firm at Hareborough that would also tender for work, and was not above cut prices. So our prices had to be so small as to be beyond competition, and my father would try to make up for that by working inordinately long hours. Then, unlike the big firms, he had no capital to enable him to buy material in the bulk, and so save costs. Then he would forget all about wear and tear to his tools, so that replacements had to come out of meagre profits. And when he had anything of a windfall or a job paid unexpectedly well, he would be generous with his money, and what was left would often not pay the bills incurred. All my young life the house was beset with travellers calling to collect accounts, and they would drive my mother almost frantic. My father would merely laugh.

[1] Any large pots.

'They'll get their money some time, won't they? Then what have you got to worry about.'

Even to their faces he would tell the travellers much the same thing, and so confident would be his assurances and so genial and genuine his manner, that he always managed to convince. But I remember one day confiding in my mother when a particularly annoyed traveller had called in my father's absence.

'When I'm a man, mother, I'm never going to have anything I can't pay for on the spot. No one's ever going to send me a bill.'

I remember she smiled at me. It must have been indeed amusing to see a boy envisaging impossible Utopias.

But the most disastrous activity in which my father ever engaged was in buying and selling horses. He had always had an eye for a horse, and from my earliest years I was used to such terms as side bones and splints. Some of our neighbours relied on him to buy horses for them, and when a certain contractor needed a dozen stout nags, my father went to London and bought them for him, and did well out of the deal. Many were greasy legged and bought for a song, but all were good enough for the job.

But that success went to my father's head, and thereafter he would go to London at intervals and pit his wits against the copers and sharpers. On one occasion he took me with him, and we went all the way by road. I remember we went to Aldridges and he bought three horses. On the homeward journey, which took two days, I had to sit in the rear of the cart and keep an eye on the horses tied behind. I remember that we stayed the night in a little inn, and when the next evening we were crossing the heaths between Barton Mills and Ouseland, I fell asleep, and when I woke I was shivering with the cold. That must have been almost fifty years ago.

A series of disasters brought those visits to an end, and never shall I forget one tragic week. He had gone to London to buy two horses only, and one was to be a fast cart nag and the other the utility kind that could pull a cart or drag a plough. For the former he was buying a cart and harness in town and driving home. At school I received a telegram telling me to meet the London train that evening and to ride home from Ouseland the other horse which had been boxed at Liverpool Street. That was a thrill for me, and I remember the porter and me going to undo the box. And there was the

horse, but doubled up in a curious way. Then we found it was
dead!

There was no compensation for that loss. I know my father
went to a solicitor and there was correspondence that added
only to the losses. As for that second nag, worse was to befall.
It was a black horse of handsome appearance, and only six
years old. By the looks of it it was worth thirty guineas and
it had cost less than half. On the journey from London it
had been a bit too skittish for his liking, and I think he was
of the opinion that it had been doped.

He decided, therefore, not to wait for a purchaser but to
send it to market with a reserve. But first he put it in our best
light trap after a day or two's rest and tried its real paces.
I went with him and we took the Shopleigh Road. That nag
fairly flew, but it was definitely hard to control. And then
came a moment I shall never forget. Suddenly it slowed and
then it went straight upright. I was pitched out at the back
of the trap and managed to roll clear. My father struck it
between the ears and it came down, and then at once it leapt
for the hedge. It cleared the hedge with the trap on one side
and itself on the other, and there it was fast. While my father
held it and soothed it, I loosened the traces and it was drawn
clear. Finally we managed to get it into the trap again, but
we let it walk all the way back.

Early the next morning my father went into the stable and
that horse was standing with a foreleg curiously limp. His
face was white as death when he came to the house for me,
and I had to drive the old pony to Attley to fetch a vet. But
here I can tell only what I remember. Some vet. may tell me
I am wrong in my terms, but this is what I understood had
happened. That horse had gone badly lame so its owner had
had it unnerved, which meant—so I gathered—that the sinews
of the foreleg concerned had been cut above and below and
then joined. Then when the lameness had temporarily gone,
the horse had been sent to Aldridges and my father had bought
it. But the joined sinews had parted irrevocably and maybe
the horse had somehow been aware of that and that had been
the cause of its behaviour. At any rate it was killed and the
knacker took its carcass. Every penny my father had raised
was gone, and my mother insisted with a vehemence such as I
had never seen her show, that never again should my father
go to London.

But that same winter he bought locally a very fine pony out of the balance of his corn money. One morning I was sent to fetch it, and I wince even now at what I saw. For that pony had tried to get out, and had got its off hind leg caught in the wire of the fence, and in trying to get free it had sawed into the flesh with results that I cannot describe. The vet. dressed the fearful wound and the pony actually recovered and could trot apparently well as ever but that monstrous scar had taken away all its value. That was bad luck, as was the loss of a fine colt that ate yew that no one knew was in a certain hedge. Providence may be on the side of the big battalions, but life as a boy was constantly reminding one that bad luck was the sure companion of the little man.

I have spoken much of my father's discipline, and I would like to show just two more facets of his character. There was that matter of not keeping his word about payments to us children, as in constant promises of a trip some day to Yarmouth. I recall in that connexion the mowing of a certain barley bottom. There was a fair crop in the middle of that field at Lammas Meadows where the pheasants and rabbits had not had time to penetrate, but unfortunately a rain had beaten it down and the grass machine had had to leave it. My father hated the idea of mopping it out himself, for he had no use for so tedious a job.

I may have indicated that all my life I have hitched my wagon to the remotest and most romantic of stars. With that strain of obstinacy that I inherited from my father, I would be infuriated and spurred on by the mere mention of impossibilities. I expect my father was aware of that when he hinted that the acre or so might have to be left as he hadn't the time to tackle it.

'I'll do it,' I told him with all the confidence of fifteen years.

'You!' he said, and his lip curled. 'I'll bet you a shilling you couldn't do it—not in a whole day.'

'I could, I'm sure I could,' I said. Then he hedged somewhat, for betting was against his principles. If I did mow it in a day I should have the shilling.

I rose before dawn, arranged with my mother that meals of sorts should be sent at breakfast, dinner, and fourses, and then got to work. Why I didn't succumb from exhaustion I still don't know, for it was mop, mop, mop, all day in the full sun, and I was no great hand at sharpening the scythe. But I was sustained by my own obstinacy, and before night fell had finished the job.

'Bravo, son,' my father said, and laughed as if the feat had been his own. But never did I see the shilling, and that was something that rankled. For if my father had set his man at that job, the cost at harvest rates would have been at least seven shillings and sixpence. And yet somehow I can see his point of view. Maybe I was in the same category of his mind as the travellers. Some day he did intend to pay me, and meanwhile he felt the intentions to be as real as the facts.

But the story I am going to relate goes deep to the mainsprings of his character. I would ask you to believe that it is not synthetic, and that things happened as I tell them, even if they depend on the memory of a twelve-year boy.

The story concerns Nell. Of all the dogs my father ever had, and he kept nothing but the best, Nell was the most lovable and the most uncannily gifted with every dog sense, and some that seemed human. Almost the most tragic day of my memory is the one when, chasing a rabbit, she ran on a carelessly thrown scythe and had to be destroyed, and to each of us it was as if something had gone from our lives that could never by any chance come back. Let me tell you some of her feats, but first let me try to show her as she was.

Nell was a little brindled bitch, with a fine strain of greyhound blood. She was small for a lurcher, and dainty and ladylike, but she had an incredible turn of speed. And she responded to more elaborate training than any dog I have known. My father would take her in the sulky[1] across the heaths, and at a suitable moment would let her go in the dusk or dark.

'Hie on, old bitch,' he would say gently as he let down the tail of the sulky, and into the dusk Nell would go. When she caught a rabbit she would actually spring with it into the back of the low cart, where my father would wring its neck and off she would go again, and that with the cart still moving. Once at a time of financial stress he took her to the heaths, and on one moonlight night she caught what he called 'sixteen grut[2] old heath rabbits', and so exhausted was she that he had to carry her home as well as that heavy load.

I have told of her feats at night netting, but it was when

---

[1] Low springless cart.   [2] Great.

we were ferreting that she showed the most uncanny skill. My father would tell her to hie on along a hedge. Into each hole would go her muzzle. If she stayed and gave a silent whimper, in that hole was a rabbit. If she moved on there was no need to put a ferret into the hole. But there was more than that. A warrener lays his ear on the ground to listen for a lined ferret at a kill some feet beneath the ground. Often that sound is too deep to locate and it is necessary to dig a series of holes to follow the direction of the line. But with Nell there was no difficulty.

'Where is't old bitch?' my father would say, and Nell would move, muzzle to ground. Where she at last stopped was the place to dig, and never do I remember my father accusing her of what might be called a lie.

Her mouth, too, was incredibly soft, so that when she snatched up a rabbit in full career the teeth never closed at all, and all the difference in that rabbit would be that its fur would be wet where she had held it. I am sure that my father loved that little bitch as he had never loved anything in his life. If he and we had starved, no money could have bought her. And she was the only one of all his dogs so superbly disciplined that he knew no petting could spoil her, and sometimes she would be allowed to come into the house where we children would stroke and fondle her. Then she would wriggle with joy and lick our hands, and faces, and her gentle eyes would be like liquid amber pools.

And so to a night when we were due on the morrow to go rabbiting at Snettley, for it was in my holidays. My father came suddenly into the house that night. My sisters were in bed and my mother sat darning at the other side of the fire.

'Didn't I tell you not to feed those ferrets?' he demanded of me.

I was astounded. I knew I hadn't to feed the ferrets for they would have to be hungry for the following day's work.

'I didn't feed them,' I said.

Then he caught me a blow on the ear that landed me across the room.

'Don't you dare tell me a lie or I'll thrash you within an inch of your life!'

'I didn't feed them,' I persisted.

'Get on up to bed,' he told me, and his hand raised so threateningly that I slipped at once through the door.

8

That night a neighbour happened to call in.

'I had some little rabbit bellies,' he said, 'so I give 'em to your ferrets as I happened to be goin' by your shed. I thowt I'd drop in and tell you so you wouldn't go feedin' 'em, only I got kept.'

When he had gone my mother was furious.

'That don't matter,' he told her, alluding to the box of the ears he had given me. 'What if he did get punished for what he didn't do? There'll be times, won't there, when he don't get punished for what he do do, and that make it right, don't it?'

In the morning my mother told me, but I remember feeling no animosity. My father said never a word; it was indeed as if nothing had happened, and off we set for Snettley. The steward there was a man whom I will call Hamford. He was a man I always liked, and though he had only one eye he was as deadly a shot as ever I've known; better even than my father. He went along with us to the brecks where we had a bit of coursing with Nell, and then we beat the gorse so that he might have a few shots, and so deadly was he that if a rabbit flashed across a few feet of ride, it was dead.

I remember that I made the fire as usual and we had our lunch in the lee of the gorse. Across to our right were arable fields, and the unfolded swedes were still there. My father knew them just the place for a squatting rabbit, so he hied Nell over. It wasn't long before Nell was back and carrying a rabbit.

'There's a good lil' old bitch,' chuckled my father. But there was something strange about Nell's approach, for it was more of a frightened sidle.

'Whuh, what's the matter with her?' he said, and got to his feet and took the rabbit out of her mouth. And no wonder she had sidled, for that rabbit had been savaged.

He stood there like a man thunderstruck. The training of months had gone in a moment. A dog with a hard mouth was useless, for every rabbit that it caught was spoilt. Then one of his mad rages seized him, and he grasped an unburnt stick from the fire. I can see the pitiful way she crouched and hear the thuds of that stick against her ribs, and then at last he cursed her away and she slunk to the hedge and lay there with that same poignant look in her eyes.

My father came to himself.

'Bast!' he said to me, 'I wouldn't have had that happen—no,

not for a hundred pound. But why'd she do it? I can't believe it.'

Food had no more taste for him and then in a minute or two Hamford came back from his lunch.

'Have you sin that old dorg of So-and-so's?' he asked us. 'I caught sight of him just now and stung his arse with a charge o' shot.'

'What dog is he?' asked my father.

'A grut black old dorg,' he was told. 'He kill no end of rabbits and either eat what he want or leave 'em lyin' about.'

He moved on with his gun till we should be ready to start again, and then my father slowly got to his feet. No wonder Nell had sidled. She had known there was something wrong with that dead but still warm rabbit she had picked up in the swedes.

Somehow he was afraid to speak but he snapped his fingers for the bitch to come. She came, low on her belly and soft eyes on his as if ready for the blow. Then suddenly he was on his knees, his cheek against the warmth of her neck. I do not know for I did not see, but yet I somehow know that where his cheek touched her soft coat, that coat was moist and warm.

Chapter IX

AN ANCIENT SCHOOL

I SHALL not burden you with a history of Ouseland or its
famous school. What matters in both are not antiquities but
those things that are flesh and blood and apprehensive. But
a paragraph or two is necessary in order to make a back-cloth
against which to view at least that school of fifty years ago.
And, as has been said, to see a movement in continuity one
must trace it to its source.

Ouseland was once a royal town and the capital of a region
vastly larger than Breckland. On its neighbouring brecks are
found the abundant flints of neolithic men, and it has what
have been claimed to be the finest Roman lines of circumvalla-
tion in Europe. At the height of its glory it had many churches
of which only three survive, and until just before the coming
of the Normans it was a cathedral city. It was only in 1094
that Herbert de Losinga removed the see finally to Norwich,
all of which you may read just inside the entrance to the present
cathedral.

But an encyclopedia of forty years ago says this:

OUSELAND. Municipal borough, Norfolk. Population (1901)
4,613.

That is all, and by it you might judge the ancient town to
be dying and almost damned, which would be very far from
the truth. But that entry is enormously misleading for its
innumerable omissions. My A.A. Handbook of 1939-40 gives
the population as about 4,000.

As for the school, the researches of my old friend George Blaydon, Ouseland's revered Town Clerk and himself an old scholar, have full uncovered its history, and it is a history which gives a somewhat parvenu air to most of our public schools. In 631, for instance, Siegbert, King of East Anglia, founded a school which could have been only at Ouseland, the one focal point of religion and education. But the town was to suffer successive burnings by the Danes, and the school did not reappear till the town's rebirth of prosperity under Edward the Confessor. When the ex-cathedral church of St. Mary the Great became a Cluniac Priory and the school was transferred to the monks—those same monks, you may recall, who preached at Heathley—Herbert de Losinga ordered it to be handed back to the secular clergy. The magnificent roll of head masters which now hangs under the arch of the old schoolroom shows an almost unbroken line until 1496.

After the Dissolution of the Monasteries, the will of Sir Richard Fulmerston directed his heirs to provide or restore a free grammar school and it is his arms that the school bears. A school was built but subsequent maladministration led to a petition by the Mayor and Corporation to James the First for redress, and the case for the school was argued by Coke, the famous lawyer, and was won. As for that building—the one that I entered fifty years ago—part of its boundary wall was that of the ancient church, and the original transept arch formed the boys' entrance to the main schoolroom. Just before my time there were some renovations, but that main building is much as it was three hundred years ago. Perhaps its most famous pupil was Thomas Paine, author of the *Rights of Man* and part framer of the American Declaration of Independence.

Among my contemporaries were the sons of the town's two lawyers, its doctors, its clergy, and its leading merchants. Disregarding the boarders, who numbered about twenty, I suppose that a good many of the parents could have sent their sons to any public school in England. They preferred, however, to send them to the ancient school of their own town, and from that school they might, or might not, proceed to a university. But there I would like to make one thing perfectly clear. There is little snobbery in my system, even if I necessarily admire the public schools. I have every reason to be grateful to a public school, for it was through my connexion with one that I was first commissioned to my county regiment, though that is a mystery I do not at the moment propose to explain. What I do abominate are those who mention such schools as if they were entitled to respect and consideration because of their mere attendance there, a respect that, if due at all, should be for the fathers that so sent them.

In my day there were between fifty and sixty pupils—or is the word scholars? The school could indeed accommodate few more, for it consisted of the one ancient room with its timbered roof and panelled walls and a more modern annexe room that led off it to the left of the great arch. In that room the lowest form—the Third—was taken, and on those rare occasions when there were set experiments in Chemistry they were staged on its table. As for the size of the main room, when I saw it after a passing of over twenty years I was amazed at its smallness, for to me it had once seemed gigantic. Now I doubt if it is much larger than the drawing-room of my house.

In it worked one master with the Fourth Porm, while the Head himself took the Fifth and the few scholars of the Sixth, all of whom did specialized work. When I ultimately reached it there were three of us: Burrows, who won a scholarship in my year and was entering the Civil Service, Neil Wilson, son of the manager of Burrell's works who was reading Greek in order to pass his university entry, and I who was working at Higher Local. A curious trio; I, about five foot something, and the others over six foot.

I have given a brief description of the Reverend Benjamin Reed. Never did one see him abroad except in his clerical dress with that immaculate topper, and he would raise it courteously even to the salutation of the humblest and grubbiest of his pupils—myself. When he made his ceremonious way from the school house between the lawns and along the path to the main porch, he was never without gown and mortar-board. An urbane, patrician figure the mere sight of whom was abundant discipline, and in all my career I can recall only the caning of one boy.

When I first entered the school there were two resident masters. Mills, whose nickname was Tubby, took the Third Form and German. He was from Gresham's School, Holt, and to me he was very much of a tyrant. My most endearing memory of him was at a certain football practice. I had been chosen and almost for the first time, as a half-back on one of the sides, and Tubby was centre-forward for the other side, and as such had been playing havoc among our defence. Then came a moment when I saw him coming down the field in full career, the ball at his toe, and that devil at my ear told me to charge him. Maybe the imagined wrongs of many months were behind me as I hurled my small body at his stomach. What happened was incredible. It was as if I had

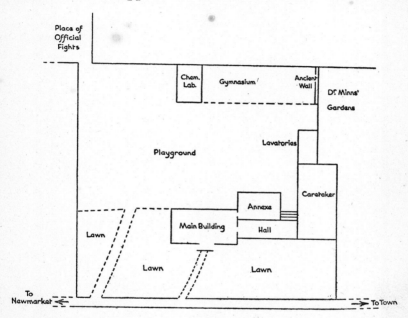

struck an immense air-cushion. Mills went straight on and I rebounded like a ball against the side of a house. As I lay half winded I was more than repaid, however, by the shout of our captain: 'Oh, well charged!'

The other master was William Owston—I am not sure of the spelling—whose nickname was Billy Boook, from his pronunciation of that word. Once I saw him stretched at full length by the side of the field recovering from a heart attack during a game, and I do not remember ever seeing him again in the field. He was a tyrant as far as I was concerned, and definitely unjust. I recall particularly an occasion when I had finished the work on hand and was reading a history book till Owston was ready to examine us, and unfortunately I had that book on my knees. Suddenly he ordered me to stand up and asked why I was not getting on with my work.

'I've finished it,' I began, and he gave me forty sums for the omission to add a *sir*.

'You were reading a book under the desk,' he said.

'Yes, sir.'

'Then take forty more sums.'

Afterwards I went up to his desk and asked if I might explain. He said I was adding insult to injury, as it were, and gave an additional forty, making a hundred and twenty in all, and I calculate that they took me six hours of slogging work.

But before you assume that I was a lamb among wolves, let me do some explaining. There is no doubt that in my first year or two at Ouseland I had none too happy a time. There was a bully of the name of Vandyke who would lambast me most unmercifully for no reason at all, and even I could see that the discipline of both Old Benn and the masters was more relaxed in the case of others than of myself. And, to be perfectly fair, there was no wonder. I was the first village scholarship boy to enter the school, and my very appearance was nothing of which the school could be proud, what with my country clothes and my hobnailed boots. As for those boots, I say again that if I had a son whose schooling had to be like my own, he would wear those same hobnailed boots. Since the school football ground in those first days was over a mile from the school, I walked each day of my life a matter of eight miles at the least, and on the roughest of roads.

I know that I have been hopelessly incapable of giving you any adequate idea of the sensation caused when I did first go to Ouseland, such a break was it with tradition. Into that fine old school whose scholars were the young aristocracy of the town and district came I, and as I have described myself, with my rusticity of dress and accent. There was the matter, too, of my having brought lunch to be eaten all by myself in the schoolroom, which must have given me in many eyes the appearance of a pariah. Then at the Speech Day which came soon after my arrival, the main speaker mentioned me, though I was blissfully unaware. He must, I think, have been a prominent Radical, for he spoke of the event my arrival at the School had been, and added most tactlessly that he hoped I should be given fair play. All that must have singled me out.

for
o put
ney.

Over the last 5 years £9,000 invested in our TESSA Plus is set to be worth £13,950°. For the full story on reinvesting, whoever your TESSA is with now, call HSBC Bank on **0800 299 299** or visit your local branch.

HSBC

YOUR WORLD OF FINANCIAL SERVICES

FOR MORE INFORMATION ON OUR PERFORMANCE PLUS ISA   RETURN THIS COUPON TO HSBC BANK PLC, FREEPOST, NWW
1502, MANCHESTER, M45 9AZ.

TITLE

SURNAME   FIRST NAME

ADDRESS

POSTCODE

DAYTIME TEL. NO. (INC STD)   EVENING TEL. NO. (INC STD)   PP1/E/95

DO YOU HOLD OTHER HSBC ACCOUNTS? ☐ YES ☐ NO (PLEASE TICK), IF SO PLEASE COULD YOU FILL IN YOUR SORT CODE
4 0 ☐ ☐ ☐ ☐ ACCOUNT NO ☐ ☐ ☐ ☐ ☐ ☐ ☐ ☐ MAY WE SEND YOU INFORMATION ABOUT OUR PRODUCTS AND
SERVICES IN FUTURE? ☐ Textphone (minicom) No 0845 712 5563. DO YOU REQUIRE THE INFORMATION IN AUDIO FORMAT? ☐

It brought me too much under the notice of authority and was the cause, maybe, of harsh discipline.

All the same it was up to me to make good, and there I had two great assets. One was a natural aptitude for games, and the other was the ability to keep my eyes and ears open and my mouth shut. When Vandyke left at the end of the first year, it was as if eternal clouds had gone and the first sun was shining, but my young policy was still to keep in the background and obey implicitly no matter what orders were given me. And so, very slowly, I found my proper place. It was not long before I perceived that justice was not harsh if one could contrive to keep altogether out of its clutches. Before the end of my second year I was a normal part of the school. I believe that by the end of the third year I was as popular as most. Indeed, I was notorious, but of that more later.

But just as an amusing indication of the tone that the Head expected from his school, let me mention the introduction of marbles. I think it was the scholarship boys from the town itself who first brought the game to the school, and for some days the Head was wholly unaware of the unclean thing, for he rarely visited the playground. Then one spring morning at Interval he did happen to have business in the Chemical Laboratory, and there in the playground were the whole of his scholars, boarders and all, crouching round rings and even kneeling on the hard earth as they played at knuckle-down or awaited their turn. At once the whole school was summoned to the main room. The Head lashed us with his scorns and threatened with his wraths if that pastime of guttersnipes appeared again. Those who had introduced it were told to stand up, and they received a special warning with hints at expulsion. My withers were unwrung, but I was sorry our orgies were to come to an end for I had been doing remarkably well.

At a quarter past nine, as you will remember, I took the train at Wortley Station. A paying day-boy from Hareborough was the only other contemporary on that train, and he was older than I, and it was not to be long before I was alone. Of Taylor, later to become an auctioneer, I remember chiefly one episode which concerned smoking. Most of the smoking of Heathley boys was done with mugwort, as we called it. One took the sere leaves, which had a chrysanthemum smell, and rubbed them in one's palms, and the result was a fibrous mass

resembling dirty cotton. Our pipes were acorn husks with
the hollow lengths of privet for stems. But Taylor introduced
me to cigarettes, and, when I was an adept, asked me if I
would like to try a pipe. The next morning he produced one
and it was one of which I didn't like the look, for all the
tobacco it held was a dry and aged dottle. But I lacked the
moral courage to refuse it, and when the dottle was lighted
I puffed away. I have never thought kindly of Taylor since then.

That train of ours would puff its way across the heaths and
halt at Rudgham to discharge passengers who would take the
Norwich train. Then it moved on across more heaths to
Ouseland, and it would be well after half-past nine when we
arrived at school, so there would be no lingering in the three-
quarter-mile walk. Almost always we took a short cut that
turned right from Station Road and emerged at St. Mary's
Church. That lane led us by Burrell's works.

Those works that lay along the river made traction engines,
road locomotives, steam wagons, and a variety of other
machinery. How many men were employed there I do not
know, but when the workmen swarmed out of the gates at
the dinner hour it seemed to me as if there must be hundreds.
I know that most of the town lived by those works, and that
there was great distress when they ultimately had to be closed
down. But I remember them chiefly because of Wilson, the
Scots manager. His sons were veritably sons of Anak, and
they were noteworthy because in their first years at school
they wore the kilt.

It would be at about ten minutes to ten when we came round
by the side path to the playground and hung our gear in the
hall. The daily papers of George Mower, cricket professional
and caretaker, would always be on his door-mat, and there was
to come a time when my duty would be to scan very hastily
the cricket scores of the previous day. That was when I was
first really aware that I had a memory, for when I got to my
form there would be at once a spate of surreptitious questions.

'How many did Surrey make?'

'How many wickets did Braund take?'

'What did Ranji get?'

'What were Yorkshire out for?'

I had to supply the answers, and I never remember being
far wrong. But while I am at memory instances, let me quote
an occasion when Burrows and I had passed a certain test and

as we had had an argument about our powers of memorizing, he asked Billy Boook to set us something to commit to memory during the remaining hour. Copies of the *Lays of Ancient Rome* were given us, and at the end of that hour I had my man well beaten, for I recited the whole of *Horatius* and a fair part of *The Battle of Lake Regilius*. A few months ago I managed to get in touch with Burrows again, and though forty years had passed since I had seen him, I recognized him at once. He was in the last year or so of his important Civil Service appointment, and had quite forgotten that episode, and that he had once boasted to me that an ancestor of his was hanged for taking part in Kett's rebellion.

Caps hung up, books taken out and hair smoothed down, we would tap at the door and enter the main-room beneath the venerable arch. Scripture would long have been over, and Old Benn would be taking Latin with the Fifth. More than once as I passed him he would frown at the sound of my hobnailed boots and audibly remark, 'Jupiter tonans!' I would pass on to the ministrations of Billy Boook and a day would have begun.

These are not the only days when the curricula and methods of schools are inextricably tied up with university requirements and examination results. At Ouseland School it was governed by the Cambridge Locals. The Third Porm was taught so that it could qualify for entry to the Fourth. The Fourth worked for the Junior Local and the Fifth for the Senior, and the Sixth might work for anything. Teaching methods were simple. As few lessons as possible were given, and those to induce the habit of private study. When you had been given this and that to learn in school or for homework, the method of testing was communal. Questions would be asked round the form, and always orally, and if you answered fifty per cent you gloated inwardly. If you fell below that standard, you wrote out all that you should have learned from twice to ten times in accordance with its length and the amount of ignorance that you had happened to display. That was the method throughout the school and I was never, except in the Sixth, to know another. End of term examinations, however, produced no punishments, but they did produce the usual reports.

Incredible as it may seem, I did Euclid—as we then called Geometry—for at least three months without having the faintest conception of what it was all about. A diagram would be put on the board and the problem run through, but it never penetrated to what lay beneath the thickness of my non-mathematical skull. It was only when I came to the notice of the Head as being too frequently in detention on Thursday afternoons, that I was able to state a case for myself. What happened between the Head and Billy Boook I do not know, but shortly afterwards it was as if I was struck by a light from heaven. I saw that Euclid actually made sense. There was even to come a time when I would amuse myself with riders to pass an odd quarter of an hour.

Scripture was to me what is known nowadays as a piece of cake. Since I liked it, and my peculiar memory functioned only for what I liked, I could romp through homework. There was the knowledge derived from my childish reading, and years of teaching by Walter Addis in Sunday school, and the fact that whenever there was a boring preacher in chapel, so much did I love the Old Testament stories that I would read them again and again, the Bible concealed by my knees. Not only did I never fail at tests, but at every Cambridge Local examination I got a distinction. And I suppose I worked less at it than any other subject.

The teaching of Chemistry during my early years was fantastic. For one thing we had no proper science master, and what happened was that we underwent a kind of super-vision in the annexe to the gymnasium that had been fitted up as a rough-and-ready sort of laboratory. But there were sinks, Bunsen burners, a few reagents and a stinks cupboard, and we were able to do the simpler experiments for ourselves. The larger ones, as the liquification of gases or the making of hydrogen by the action of sodium on water, were set pieces performed perhaps once or twice a term. What the most cunning of us did was to manufacture fireworks from mixtures that always included potassium chlorate. Once I helped my-self to a piece of sodium and put it in a special bottle. I was intending to take it home to make hydrogen with jam jars as apparatus, and thereby to mystify my sisters, and also impress. But it so happened that that summer night I got a ride from the station in Sam Smith's coal-cart. As we drew near the Reed Pit the devil whispered at my ear.

'One thing we learn at school,' I suddenly announced, 'is how to set water on fire!'

'Bast! don't you tell me that,' said Sam with a grin. 'I reckon I can swaller a good deal, but darn it, I ain't a-goin to ha' that.'

We were abreast of the pit and I uncorked my bottle and threw it. Liquid and sodium came out in the flight and then suddenly the water was in flame.

'Whuh, what the davvul!' said Sam, eyes bulging.

It took a few moments before he recovered and then he wanted details. I maintained an esoteric reserve, but before that night had gone most of the village must have heard, and most, I am sure, thought it was Sam who was the liar.

German I always disliked, for it was exceedingly badly taught. The pronunciation was execrable and till I left school I was pronouncing *der* as *durr*, and *des* as *dezz*. About gutturals Mills was specially hazy, but as there was never any oral work it mattered little. Later the set books were far too advanced. In the course of five years I made my way—chiefly alone— through *Die Journalisten*, Schiller's *Wilhelm Tell*, and Goethe's *Autobiography*, and I remember never a word of any one of them. Whether I passed or not in the various examinations I very much doubt. But about that German I can tell quite a good story against myself.

I was at Heliopolis in 1918 when some German prisoners happened to come in. I had just taken the paroles of some senior Turkish generals in French, so the Colonel sent for me and asked if I also spoke German. Then off I went to interrogate those prisoners. But when I began to frame my first question, I realized that in only fourteen or so years I had forgotten every word I had ever learned. I could not even have asked one of those men what his name was, or his age, so utterly blank was my mind. It was a frightening feeling suddenly to be tongue-tied and there was what the Colonel would say when I reported back. Then I had a brainwave. Did any man speak French? I asked in French. One prisoner did, and was forthwith made interpreter. But that the Colonel was never to know.

English was my passion. There memory was on my side, and I discovered that what John Balfour had taught me was much in advance of my form. But the greatest of joys was when at last I came to the Fifth and was taught by the Head. A play of Shakespeare was then included in the curriculum, and the Head would sit in front of the form while we read a part in turn. Occasionally he would pause for some explanation, and sometimes he would take a part himself, but to me those hours were a sheer delight and I would wish that each hour could linger itself out.

And there my memory so helped me that it was never long before I had a play by heart. I would even read notes and introduction in my spare time, and once before an examination I committed to memory all the glossary. It was during one of those Shakespeare readings that I heard for the first time Old Benn burst into laughter before a class. *Julius Cæsar* was the play, and we were near the end of the hour. Old Benn himself was taking the part of Brutus.

> Bru.   *Peace! Count the clock.*
> Cas.   *The clock hath stricken three.*
> Treb. 'Tis time to part.*

And at that very second the clock above the porch entrance struck three o'clock. A happy coincidence, but it was typical of that teaching of Shakespeare at its best that Old Benn should have laughed and we should have laughed, for in no other lessons of my remembering could it have happened.

I have said that I had an aptitude for games, but it was to be a considerable time before I was admitted to even a junior practice. I was small, for one thing, and my policy, as I said, was to remain as inconspicuous as possible till I had at least got some sort of bearings. To me the senior boys of the school were like men: the Lawrences from Bury St. Edmunds, Bishop, the elder Wilsons and the head of the school, a boy named Legget. When he left, word went round that he was playing cricket for London County, the side that played under Grace when the old man retired from more serious cricket. Little did I think that I should play against Grace myself. Upon that memorable scene I nothing common did or mean, but I did nothing else. Grace was dismissed cheaply, but I had no hand in it, nor in anything else that mattered.

Where I first began to become noticed was in that open gymnasium of ours, with its concrete floor. We did sporadic exercises there under Mills with the only apparatus parallel bars and a horizontal bar, though later there was a vaulting-horse and mat. But I never shone at gymnastics; where I soon began to excel was at the special game of football that was played there in every possible leisure moment, even in summer. It would be with a tennis ball, and as in that confined space there might be as many as fifteen a side, one had to learn to dribble a ball round a threepenny piece. There was the art of kicking that ball against the one wall and trapping it on the rebound, and it was that ball control that made me whatever footballer I was to become. My small size was an advantage, too, for I had to learn to avoid charges. A grand game that! And if that gymnasium had not disappeared· long since, I would drop in some day and show the modern boy that he had no monopoly of tricks.

But having praised myself to that extent, it might be as well to show another side to the picture. For the first three years of my school life, a Thursday afternoon was a time to dread. There were the things that I found hard to assimilate; there was my memory that played me tricks in things that I did not like, there were the temptations of the Wortley Road that kept me from a last revision of homework, there were the excitements of the train and there was in addition a kind of lethargy of despair that would get the better of me.

It was the custom of a master to have on his desk a list of detentions. If one's name were on that list at four o'clock on a Thursday afternoon, then one stayed in school till nearly six o'clock, until, in fact, there was just time to catch the train. As my name would appear several times on that list, and indeed on the lists of more than one master, I never knew what it was to play games on a Thursday afternoon. Sometimes I had not removed my name from all the sheets when a quarter to six arrived, which meant a kind of hangover till the following week, and it was that accumulation that brought a hopelessness. Or one might be ordered to have the list cleared by the Monday, which meant working at home during a week-end, and I was never allowed to put pen to paper on a Sunday.

But then came my conversion, as miraculous to me as that spiritual change that was the basis of Methodism. The first impulse came from a noteworthy happening. At just below my age I had sat for the Cambridge Junior, and when the results came out I found I had passed with distinctions in Religious Knowledge and English. But that was no great matter. Burrows, who had a much better brain than mine, had at least three distinctions, for he was good at science and mathematics, and for the latter, except Euclid, I had no brain at all. Indeed, once algebra arrived at permutations and combinations, my mind refused to function, and the rest of algebra might have been so much gibberish. Logarithms I liked, but trigonometry in the mass might, after the first few elementary chapters, have been Arabic script. In my last year I was given Loney's *Spherical Trigonometry* and told to get on with it. When I sat for the examination I left the room with my paper unsullied by a single word or figure.

A few days after the publication of those first examination results I arrived at school one morning and no sooner did I appear than the school was called to the main-room. When we were all assembled the Head made an announcement, and to my amazement he mentioned my name. A pupil of the school, Home by name, had come out at the head of the list of all the candidates for Junior Local English, and that throughout England and the Empire. The Head therefore declared the day a holiday in honour of the event and the school would dismiss forthwith. I know that I bolted at once for the station where I had to await the midday train.

But to me everything had no reality. I had designedly done nothing, and how can one rejoice at what has never been anticipated or even envisaged. In fact I said nothing at home except that we had been given a holiday, and it was not till the arrival of a monetary reward that my mother was aware of what had happened. Then John Balfour had to be told, and I remember how ashamed I was for fear some boy at school should see his laudatory contributions to the *Ouseland and Hareborough Times*.

Providence in its ways is said to be inscrutable. Some would prefer to say that chance is a queer thing, but I have often looked back and wondered at the trivial or eccentric happenings that have somehow always shaped my life, even to that fantastic moment when, in some odd fit of cussedness, I told myself I would write a novel. Take the train of events, and how that solitary and precocious life with my aunt had made me a reader of anything on which I could lay my hands. There was that knowledge of *Pilgrim's Progress* that contributed to the winning of that original scholarship, and might have been the vital factor. There was the fact that in our village was a man like John Balfour and another like Walter Addis. To look back at all those things is to have a strange humility.

But that examination result somehow changed all my outlook, and there came a time when like Saul of Tarsus I was suddenly at the parting of the ways. Where or when it was I do not know, but I can remember as vividly as if it were only yesterday how all at once I took stock of myself. Why should those Thursday evenings be a continual drudge and dread, and my week-ends given up to the writing of interminable detentions? Surely, it suddenly seemed, those two years had been lunacy of the worst. By skimping homework that would have taken no more perhaps than twenty minutes to half an hour, I had consistently given myself punishments that lasted many times as long. That didn't make sense. And yet there was the simple and unanswerable fact, and as soon as I saw that for myself it was as if, like Christian, I had had a great burden rolled from my back.

When I returned to school it was with a new resolve, and in some queer way my memory served me even better, for I learned to trust far less to memory than to sheer application. Not that I became anything of a model pupil. Except in that matter of profit and loss I was what I had always been. In fact I probably became as notorious for devilry and mischief as any pupil of my generation, but the details of that deserve a chapter to themselves.

Chapter X

MUSICAL INTERLUDE

SINCE a musical interlude is defined as a short piece played between the acts of an opera or drama, its use as a chapter heading seems on reflection something of a misnomer. But music was always to play a considerable part in my young life, and it is only right and seemly to acknowledge the fact. When now in my middle age it has become something of a passion, it is more than seemly to pay at least some tribute to those to whom I owe an infinity of pleasure.

As one who in his unregenerate days was ejected forcibly from the Old Oxford and was familiar with the old-time music-hall and its giants of comedians, I can scarcely be accused of being a highbrow. But in that same early manhood I also haunted the Albert Hall and Queen's Hall, and stood in the queue for the gallery at Covent Garden and later saw every opera produced at the original Stoll. Even now, though my use of the wireless is for symphony concerts, Itma, and the news, I would still listen to the jokes of the stock comedians had I not heard them forty years ago.

But I do not give myself airs for the musical tastes I happen to possess. I mention them only to show what a far cry it is to that first musical experience which I so vividly remember. My aunt presented me with a mouth-organ, and a nurse—or was it a governess?—allowed me to go to the very bottom of the garden for the opening performance. I think I was between five and six, for I could read fluently, and that was why I was told that with the instrument in its case was music to play. I took out that music and unfolded it and then put the mouth-organ to my lips. I wonder if you can appreciate the utter blankness that came to my young mind when nothing happened, for I must have imagined that that printed sheet was some magic that would automatically make the music flow. As far as I remember, I at once proceeded to yell with vexation and grief.

I do not remember music in my aunt's house and the first band that I heard play was at Fenwold, though I forget what the occasion was. But I do remember that I was told to look out for the passing of the Duke of York and his newly married wife, then on their honeymoon, I believe, and staying at Didlington Hall. I remember the royal couple driving past in an open carriage, and that memory came vividly back because this chapter was written on the Sunday of victory celebrations when Queen Mary returned from the West Country to be present at the service at St. Paul's.

Practically every memory of my young days at Heathley is full of music. I have mentioned elsewhere the German bands, the band that accompanied the Friendly Societies on their Whit-Sunday church parades, and how crowds would assemble from near and far to listen to its playing on the Mound. There was the harp and flute from Hareborough that played during the Friendly Societies' annual suppers in the school, and there were the accordions that made the music for our homely dances. Among the boys the tin whistle was the solo instrument, and there was that special whistle belonging to the young shepherd which also seemed to me must possess magical powers, though when I acquired it, it made my own efforts no more easy.

My father performed upon the piccolo, and sometimes of an afternoon he would fetch that instrument from the bedroom, take it out of its case and then practice in the parlour by himself. More fearsome was the accordion owned by a neighbour—a young keeper—and his hour for playing was immediately after Sunday dinner, and as he was an indifferent performer and had the smallest of repertoires, the maddening drone of it would infuriate my father when about to take his short pre-service nap. The village also had its concertinas, but the only English one that I heard played was owned by a neighbouring parson, who performed on it at a vicarage fête for some charity. To me it was a revelation, especially the harmonies in the bass, and as a musical event it was a Heathley sensation.

From our earliest years we took part in family singing. Maybe that was some Puritan survival of that love of communal music-making in Tudor and Stuart times and which was a passion with Pepys. I do not know if the Victorian practice yet survives, but to me there was no more delightful aspect of family life. It was my father who was the mainspring, and his was the book of anthems and religious pieces, attempts at which were a kind of ultimate reward. But generally we sang the old hymns of Methodism, with my father showing a preference for those that had a fine rolling bass. My mother preferred *Rockingham* and *Sandon*. She would lend a treble, and we others would take such parts as were within our compass and abilities to read music. But rarely did such an evening end without at least an attempt to render *Vital Spark*, of which my father was particularly fond. In chapel, too, we learned to take our parts, drowned though they would be by the lusty voices of the congregation, except perhaps in the thinner congregations of an afternoon.

When I changed from child to boy and was allowed a short walk after evening service, I would often go on moonlight walks with three companions, and as soon as we were out of the village we would sing, for that small company had somehow chosen itself as something of a quartet. Mine was nothing of a voice, so I would take the contralto part, and we had also a bass, a tenor, and a boyish baritone for the treble. It was always the hymns of Methodism that we would sing, and you can imagine our gratification when a nieghbour once told us how he looked forward to hearing our voices coming across the fields on the clear air of those Sunday nights.

An event to which we children would always look forward was the coming to tea of Mrs. Addis, who gave music lessons to my sisters. Her playing was to us that of a virtuoso, what with the amazing rapidity of her fingers and the rapt harmonies that came from the instrument. Never did one of those performances end without my making a request. It was for—of all things—*God Save The Queen*. But it was a special setting, to be found in the then Methodist Hymnal, with the national anthem repeated four times, and at the end of each it would subtly modulate into another key. It was those modulations that had for me a thrill and romance.

But the most wonderful music for me in those days was the church organ. I imagine that Maud Pardon was no great performer, but then I was no critic. All I knew was that the church organ had sonorities infinitely beyond those of the pedal organ of the chapel. What I liked above all was the hymn *Come Holy Ghost, Our Souls Inspire,* as rendered in church on those Whit-Sunday afternoons when I visited it as a young Oddfellow. I think it was the minor key that so appealed to me. And now I come to look back I seem to be sure that all our Methodist hymns were in the major, and that congregational singing had in it much of rejoicing. Minors were rare with us and frequent in church, and it was the rare rather than the usual that made its appeal.

You may recall that bicycle ride to Leicestershire. My cousin Edith, who also had the Home love of music, arranged for us to go to Leicester Opera House where the Moody-Manners Company happened that week to be performing. That was a revelation to one so young and rustic as myself. I remember we stood in the queue for the early doors, and the building, when I entered it, was overpowering. Maybe if I saw it now—if it exists—I should think otherwise, but I have never seen it since and I prefer to see it through the eyes of that first night.

But what I recall most nearly is the moment when the orchestra began the overture to *Maritana*. I had never heard anything even faintly resembling an orchestra and I thought I was listening to a church organ, which was the nearest I could come at comparison.

The plot of *Maritana* was easy for me, even then, to follow, and its melodies naturally made an immediate appeal. A night or so later we saw *Carmen*, which was a vastly different proposition. I admit I was fascinated, but there was much that I did not understand in the plot, and the music, however enthralling, was naturally above my young head. But it is curious that that night I should have listened to the most famous Carmen of all time—Zélie de Lussan. I never saw her again, and when I saw other Carmens, my own memories were too shallow and insecure to make possible comparison for myself.

I have said that my sisters had music lessons from Mrs. Addis, and how the money—little though it might be—was found is again a matter for the imponderables. I was exempt from those lessons and humdrum scales and exercises, though

later I took up the violin. But what I chiefly remember was
the rendering by my eldest sister of one of those pieces called
descriptive, which were so popular at the end of the last
century. Her *chef-d'œuvre* was one descriptive of the South
African War, and I can still see that piece of music with its
pom-pom bass of accompaniment and the massed bass chords
that told of cannon. There was the departure of the troops,
the arrival, the battle, and finally the return to the strains of
Home, Sweet Home. I believe I was very impressed, and why
not? Programme music even of that naïve type has in it the
appreciation of better things.

Once a year the handbell players from a neighbouring village
would pay us a visit. My father would look forward to their
coming, but the first time I heard them I was depressingly
disappointed, and maybe at the thinness of their harmonies.
Most of my father's pleasure, I am sure, was due to their being
a link with his own boyhood. To me the performance was
interesting and no more. Of greater interest were the players,
some of whom wore the top hats suitable for the occasion,
and most of whom were bewhiskered. But there were no
ringers at Heathley church, for it had only a single bell. Maybe
there had been a full peal before the original tower fell into
ruin, but that one bell was important enough to us in the
village, for the clerk would take pains to begin its ringing at
the precise second and Heathley would adjust its clocks and
watches to its sound.

The village possessed no notable singers except perhaps
John Balfour, who had a fine baritone. But I remember when
for some function in the chapel a special singer came, and she
was brought, I believe, by one of the more well-to-do of our
local preachers with whom she was staying or of whom she
was a relation. The chapel was packed to hear her and I
remember afterwards, when I or one of my sisters remarked
on something unique in her voice, at least in our small
experience, that my mother reminded us that she had been
'trained'. What the term implied we did not know, but I do
know that it vaguely became in our young minds something
of a standard. I remember an outspoken friend of the family
remarking of my sister that she had quite a good voice, considering that it wasn't trained.

At Heathley school we did tonic sol-fa, and for the life of
me I cannot think why, even in rural schools, such training is

still persisted in. To me it seems as easy and more valuable to begin at once with what I might call normal music. I had no great aptitude, especially for the things for which I had no particular liking, but I picked up the reading of music at second-hand from my sisters, and by myself. But maybe it is more convenient to hang on the wall a chart of tonic sol-fa and by the use of a pointer to induce the dullest witted to respond.

But at Ouseland my musical education really began, even if we were assumed to have learned music for ourselves. I was never in time for morning prayers, and I was always impatient for afternoon prayers to be over, so that I could be away to football or cricket, and yet when I look back at those school-days, the nearest memories are of those evening hymns. Old Benn had a fine tenor and his voice would sound above us all. Later when our voices broke, some of us would sing bass, and I remember the Head's pleased acquiescence when I asked to join their company.

Billy Boook was our usual accompanist on the piano that stood by the great arch to the right of the head master's desk, but I know now that the limit of his musical ability was the playing of our hymns. But on Fridays we had a visiting music-master, who was usually the organist of the ex-cathedral church of St. Mary the Great. The one I chiefly remember was B.—that is all I am certain of about his name—for I was particularly impressed on learning that it was from him that Maud Pardon was having lessons. I remember him, too, as a fine footballer, for all our music-masters played games with the school. When he left us it was to take up an appointment as organist and choirmaster at the cathedral city of Bridge-town, capital of the Barbados.

Hemsley was perhaps the most notable of them all, for he was the first music-master we had seen who looked the part. B. looked and dressed like an ordinary master, except that he wore no gown, but Hemsley, who had studied, I believe, in Germany, had a superb head of hair and, though quite young even in our eyes, wore a velvet jacket and a flowing black tie. And I chuckle even to-day when I think of those afternoons when he played the hymns at evening prayers.

But I was wrong to say he played the hymns. What he played was an accompaniment or variation on a theme, and he played even those with a difference. Now those hymns were to Old Benn—and I say it charitably—a something in which he with his tenor took the leading part. But Hemsley did more than steal his thunder. What he would do was virtually to bring the congregational singing to an end, so engrossed would we be with his playing. For he gave to those performances the mannerisms of the concert hall, with dexterous overhands, and hands poised high above the instrument ready to descend. There were subtle descants on the bass or more florid ones on the upper reaches, and the intricacies of his harmonies were ravishing to the ear. Meanwhile our voices would sink lower and lower as we became engrossed in those performances, and Benn would be looking disapprovingly in the direction of the piano, and as a mark of that disapproval his voice would cease. And yet he could never have spoken to Hemsley on the matter, for those Friday performances continued throughout the period of that master's stay. And in case you should think of Hemsley as something of a poseur or namby-pamby, let me add that he was a first-class outside-left, and the best fast bowler we boys had ever met.

I remember an afternoon when we happened to be reading Milton with the Head.

> . . . *many a winding bout*
> *Of linked sweetness long drawn out*

was what Sammy Greenhill happened to read. The Head halted him for questioning.

'What's the meaning of that, Greenhill?'

Sammy thought for a moment or two.

'Please sir, it's like when Mr. Hemsley plays the piano on Fridays.'

A quick frown passed across Old Benn's face, and Sammy was curtly told that it was an inappropriate answer. But I wonder.

Under those music-masters we were introduced to fine choral music. B. was organizing in the town a performance of Gaul's *Holy City*, then much in favour, and we had to learn the choruses at school so that selected voices could take part. With Hemsley we did a choral setting of *The Lay of the Last Minstrel*, though by whom I have forgotten, even if I can still hum the opening bars. But I remember that work because it led to a detention and my absence from a match which I would have given much to see. My Uncle Frank had a dry humour, and he was responsible for a parody of the opening lines of Scott's poem from which I was unlucky enough to quote:

> The way was long, the wind was cold,
> The minstrel was infernal old.

The boy to whom I whispered them that Friday afternoon had too keen a sense of humour, and guffawed, and that drew attention to myself.

One other thing I recall about Hemsley, which was that he opened the pipe organ at Ouseland Primitive Methodist Chapel. What I imply is that he gave an opening recital, which was billed throughout the town and district. One item was in big type on the bills—Mendelssohn's *War March of the Priests*. Vague ideas from Rider Haggard's Aztecs and from Hebrew history so worked on my young mind that I could think of nothing but that march, and finally I got permission to stay for the night with friends so as to be present at the recital. The recital at last began, but I was waiting for the imagined barbaric splendours of that march. Then at last I whispered to some one next to me who had a programme, and was shown the item that at the moment was being played. It was then that I realized that the march for which I had been waiting almost in agony had been the opening item.

As the result of the educational and pioneering work of those masters in Ouseland, a Musical Society was founded, and works like *Elijah*, *St. Paul*, and *Acis and Galatea* were performed with visiting singers for solo parts. To clinch what I have only implied as to Heathley's love of music, may I say that at least three young men from Heathley Chapel would ride all those lonely and bitter winter miles across the heaths to attend practices, and that whatever the weather and the fact that they could rarely reach home again till half-past ten at night.

But my happiest musical Ouseland memory was a concert given by the school in conjunction with the town Musical Society. One part—and for the life of me I cannot say whether it was the first or the second—was given up to that performance of *Acis and Galatea*, and I know that among the visiting soloists was Miss Kate Cherry. But the other parts were provided entirely by the school, and there the only item that I remember was given by a friend of the Head who came down from London especially to entertain us. Those were the days of the great entertainers at the piano, like Corney Grain, and this particular man was such a performer, and first-class. Again and again he was called back to the platform, but what I remember—at this moment I can hum the tune—was a song of his with a chorus that ran something like

Oh - I - o - o - Oh - i - - o,
There was a little nigger and he wouldn't grow no bigger,
And he lived on the banks of the Ohio.

That, for me, was the high-light of the evening. Maybe it shows why one who was to hear Busoni and Carreño, Kubelik, Melba, and Alma Gluck was also spiritually at home at most music-halls. But the only other thing I recall about that night was that it was the first time I actually slept at the school. I was too tired to remember much about the dormitories, but I do know that in the morning there was the unpleasant surprise of pre-breakfast prep. And that brings us back to the school again.

Chapter XI

AN ANCIENT SCHOOL—*continued*

As a result of that examination I had been awarded a further scholarship. Fortunately it was a more valuable one or I might never have been able to take it up. But the amount awarded was now sufficient to pay school fees and books and train fares as before, and there was a surplus that would pay for lunches at the school-house and help with my clothes.

To me it is absolutely incredible that I should have been kept at Ouseland during those first years, which were, as I have related, nothing but a series of financial crises. Even the little money that I could have earned would have made a difference, but as it was I was very much of a cuckoo in the family nest. Since my clothes had risen to the standard of my former Sunday ones, they cost far more, and as there was no brother below me to take them over when I grew out of them, they became almost a dead loss. Not that I grew fast or often. When I left home I was five foot two, and during the next six months I shot up another four and and half inches, a height that made me easily the tallest of the family. But that, as they say nowadays, had become my personal headache.

How my mother pinched and scraped on my behalf I shall never know. But she had good friends behind her, at least in spirit—John Pardon and John Balfour who would insist on my having my chance. But what none of them knew was that school was costing far more than was paid for by that original scholarship. When reports arrived at the end of a term there would be a bill enclosed with small amounts as extras, and they alone must have upset every financial calculation, but there was more to it than that.

Cricket and football clothes had to be bought and to those I could sometimes contribute by spare-time work. But as soon as I got into one of the elevens there were monies for brake and railway fares, and since the schools we played were as far afield as Norwich, North Walsham, and Ely, it was up to me to see that I somehow paid for myself and did not allow such costs to appear on an end of term bill. That was where my poaching stood me in good stead. More than once I brought pheasants in my satchel and sold them to an Ouseland dealer. Late in the evenings I would be abroad—unknown to my mother but to the knowledge of and maybe with the tacit consent of my father—with the stripped gun about my person, ready to assemble it when a shot presented itself. Many a time I would be up at three in the morning and out on brecks and heaths waiting for a dawn shot.

Elsewhere I have discussed the ethics of poaching, and I repeat that to me there was nothing dishonest in such matters, even if I did have to run the desperate gauntlet of keepers. Radicals principles and our own sufferings under the Game Laws made poaching not only a righteous cause but something of a crusade. All the better then if it was profitable at the same time. And it is noteworthy that always to me a theft—except perhaps from an orchard—would have been unthinkable. But though I ascribed my escapes from keepers to my own skilful planning and execution, I know now that Field at least was often aware of what was going on, and I like to think that he understood and sympathized with the predicament in which I was finding myself.

Only once was I actually caught red-handed. It was on a summer evening and I had been to Lammas Meadows to shoot a rabbit for the pot. As I came home I saw just inside the Park two fine young rabbits feeding, and I got them both with one shot. At once I nipped through the hedge and had them, and in the same moment I caught sight of a keeper's hat just visible above the hedge past which he was running. But in that hedge was a curious kind of hollow that I had discovered, so I crawled into it and there lay hidden. In a moment or two the keeper was looking for whoever had fired that shot. I could hear him muttering to himself as he wondered why nobody was in sight, and then I heard him give an 'Ah!' I peeped out and saw to my horror that when I had nipped into that hiding-place I had forgotten to take the gun!

'You needn't touch that gun, Harry,' I said, and to his amazement the mysterious voice was followed by myself. And what a stroke of luck it was that the keeper should have been a member of our newly formed Heathley football team, of which I was part member, part coach. What happened it is not fair to say, but if ever Harry is in need of a small loan, I tell him here and now that he has only to ask for it.

My mother must have been relieved that there were no more lunches to pack for me, and, since I should be having a good meal at school, no need to prepare a hot tea for me at night. Also I had always been given a penny with which to buy a cake to help down my bread and butter or bread and cheese, though it is true that I never bought a cake in my life but saved the pennies for emergencies. But I had come to like those solitary lunches in the classroom and in course of time there was another boy that joined me. After we had had our frugal meal we would read the books that we found in a kind of cupboard in the panelling, and some were vast black-letter folios that must have dated from soon after Caxton, or we would have a private game of football with a tennis ball.

Above the door through the entrance arch hung the school crest, glazed and in a frame. One day a lofted kick caught that glass fair and square and it shattered. We gathered up every piece and even then the jagged remains hung to the frame which was far too high for us to reach. So with infinite precautions we fetched the ladder with which George Mower cleaned the windows, and the jagged pieces were removed. That was my first lesson in camouflage, for the absence of the glass was never discovered in all my remaining time.

At school lunches I lost a good many rough edges. I do not mean that there was a vast collection of knives, forks, and spoons of which to learn the nice manipulation, but since Old Benn presided and all masters ate with us, I did at least learn table manners and something of carving, not that the manners of our family meals had anything of the crude or boorish. Just what I learned I cannot explain, but I do remember the pauses in a meal when Old Benn would talk and we were expected to listen. It might be about the events of the time

or some local affair, but it made the table something beyond
a mere convenience for a hearty and hasty meal.

A few years ago I happened to be in a place where my name
was mentioned and a young man came up to me and confirmed
that my name was what it was. Then he told me he was an
Old Fulmerstonian. A modern word, by the way. In my day
it was Old Ouselandian.

'Didn't I use to hate your name, sir,' he said.

'*My* name?'

'Yes,' he said. 'You were always being held up as an
example of what we might do if we put our backs into it.
You were a sort of criterion. And a bit of a bogy.'

I was horror-struck by that revelation. How such a per-
verted legend could have arisen I did not know. And I was
vastly annoyed. It was bad enough to have my sisters in my
own house and gardens keeping their children from mischief
by the threat of my name, but this was something far worse.
For the whole thing was built on false premises. In fact, it
was preposterous, even if I found an ironic satisfaction in
contemplating what might have happened at Ouseland if my
successors had slavishly followed my various examples.

But I had no remedy. I could not very well write to the
then head master and make my sober protest, for, as in the case
of the lady, it might have been thought that I was protesting
too much. And then an opportunity presented itself. I
received a letter from the Head asking me to come down on
Speech Day and distribute the prizes, but I happened to be on
Service at the time and had to refuse. Two years ago the
request was renewed, and on the plea that the school wished
to do me honour! I did my best to remove that misunder-
standing and when my rightful position was established, I did
go to Ouseland; I had my chance and I meant to take it.

I did not utter the words of a grave and reverend signor.
What I did, at least in the beginning, was to save future
generations of Fulmerstonians from my name. I told them
the truth, and the germ of it lay in the true story with
which I began.

When early in the last war I was due to go to France,
some impulse drove me to a sight of my old school again. I
was in uniform, and Mrs. Mower, who showed me round, was
wholly unaware of my identity. I thanked her when we were

parting and ventured to give her a tip, with the request that she should buy herself some small souvenir.

'And what might your name be, sir?' she asked the young officer.

'Home,' I said.

'Home!'

There came over her face a look of the most diabolical hatred. It was frightening in its malignancy.

'Home!' she said again. And then, with a fierce intensity: 'You were a bad 'un, you were!'

So there at last was the truth, even if that truth was slightly emphasized. And the simple explanation was that as soon as I became assimilated, as it were, into the school, and recognized by something of merit as a natural part of it, I once more became myself. That self had always been adventurous. That self loved risks for their own sake and hated the humdrum and monotonous.

But part of Mrs. Mower's dislike arose from the affair of the huge mince-pie. This was of dinner-plate size, and another boy and I shared it, but first we induced Mrs. Mower to heat it up for us. No sooner had I wolfed my large portion, which was in the comparative secrecy of the hall and after school hours, than my stomach rebelled, and forthwith I ejected the whole of that monstrous meal on the tesselated floor. It was Mrs. Mower who had to clean up and she must have had no great liking for me from that moment on. As for myself, I have never touched a mince-pie since.

And there was the affair of the horse-chestnut. I had two or three of them in my pocket and was exhibiting them to some boy or other, when George Mower happened to pass us in the playground on the way to his house. The devil was at my ear and just as George was about to turn into the passage-way I let fly. But I had forgotten my skill at throwing, and that horse-chestnut caught him clean in the back of the neck. In a flash I whipped my hand back into my pocket but I was too late. George came back and took me personally to the Head. He used the Potterian phrase of having had his eye on me for some time, and the horse-chestnut was therefore only a kind of culmination. I wasn't caned, but I was threatened with expulsion.

And maybe because that affair followed so soon on the case of the infatuated artist. It had been a wet day and therefore there were no games. I did my homework after school and then went to the station where I had still over an hour to wait. It was bitterly cold and the station was deserted, so I sat over the waiting-room fire. After a time I noticed that the poker had been left in the fire and when I pulled it out it was red-hot. It was also pointed conveniently for use. As for material, there were the painted sides of the fire-place, so I got at once to work. I do not know what scrolls and arabesques I shaped—but I know I did a good job. Too good, as you will see.

Two mornings later I was called before the Head.

'Was it you, Home, who disfigured the lintels of the mantelpiece at the railway station?'

'Yes, sir,' I said.

But what puzzled me was how that mischief could have been definitely ascribed to me, for the station was used by day boys from all along the Norwich and London lines and the Bury line too. And I was positive that nobody had seen me in the waiting-room. But when I reached that waiting-room that evening and surveyed the scene of my crime, there was the solution. So creditable in my eyes had been that decorative work, and so infatuated indeed had I been with it, that I had added my initials beneath!

Many years later, Mr. Cole, the then head master, spent with his family an afternoon at my Heathley house and I asked them to bring with them George Mower, and George duly came. He and my father talked about cricket while we others played tennis, and then at tea I reminded George about the horse-chestnut. It pleased him enormously.

'How'd you know it was me, George?' I asked him.

'I didn't,' he said. 'I thought it was another boy at first, and then I remembered how you'd often hit a stump at thirty yards and more. Then when I came up to you, your face went red.'

And that goes to show. But about that regrettable time there was also the famous fight which I had with Charles Sayer *alias* Bumper. It arose through the singing of the *British Grenadiers* on a Friday afternoon, for when we came to the line

Then let us fill our bumper and drink a health to those . . .

we would make a natural fortissimo and look pointedly at Bumper. That particular afternoon his angry eye fell on me, and when we came out of school he struck me. I struck back and a fight was forthwith arranged, and with the full etiquette of a ring and seconds. Neil Wilson was my second, and that fight took place on the waste ground towards the Brandon Road.

Now Bumper was almost six foot and I was then about five foot at the most. I went in with body blows and a neat one in the solar plexus doubled Bumper up and brought his chin within reach. Neil told me to go in and finish him and my supporters round the ring were yelling the same, but somehow I could not bring myself to hit a helpless opponent, and quixotically I let Bumper recover. Then it became a test of endurance between my nose which his long arm continued to prod, and his stomach which more than once I managed to catch with an upper-cut. I had him doubled up again and again could not bring myself to land a *coup de grâce*, and then when his long reach had almost worn me down, George Mower appeared and we scattered and ran. In the morning Bumper and I appeared before the Head. I think it was the fact that we had been stripped to our waists in true pugilistic style and that my nose had been bleeding, that was the shock to the Head and brought me into ill-repute.

'Fighting like two young cannibals, they were, sir,' was part of George's evidence and it helped to get us a gating for a fortnight. But he was a good fellow was Bumper, and a fighter to the last. On the Roll of Honour in that old classroom, now the School Library, you can read his name.

Though the Head was never aware of it, some of us, including myself, followed the fortunes of race-horses. That was because Musker of Shadwell Court was a notable owner, and some boys had seen over the stables. I remember I would look at the racing news in George Mower's paper to see if a horse of Musker's had won, and I recall a bitter spring day when we were playing a match at Norwich and I invested a precious halfpenny in an evening paper to see what had won the Two Thousand Guineas, and the depression that fell on some of us when we saw in the stop press that Henry the Fifth—or was it the First?—had run only second.

Some of the senior boys would boast of making bets, but my gambling career—happily cut short—began as a layer when Neil Wilson dared me to take his bet on the Autumn Double—the Cambridgeshire and Cesarewitch. I always rose to a challenge, but was cautious enough to ask the amount of his proposed bet. He suggested a shilling.

'Bet you a shilling then,' I said, and asked for the names of his horses.

'The two favourites,' he told me, and that took the wind clean out of my sails, for in the very word favourite there was something ominous to myself. Then when I appreciated the mathematics of a double and realized that I might have to pay as much as two or three pounds, my days were spent in the blackest of despairs. On the afternoon of the first race I made an excuse not to play football and when the Norwich train came in I bought an evening paper. The favourite had been nowhere, and a monstrous burden rolled from my back. I did not even rejoice that I had won a shilling; indeed I do not remember ever receiving it.

Memory plays queer tricks. Why is it, for instance, that I recall few of the important events of my schooldays? Of the impact on us of the South African War I recall only a holiday after the Relief of Mafeking, Old Benn reading Kipling to us, and the faces of British generals on the cigarette cards of the period. I scarcely remember that procession when the school marched to the Town Hall for the Proclamation of Edward the Seventh, and I only faintly remember the stir when the King would come to Elveden to shoot. Then there were the speakers, including a bishop, who presented the prizes, but of whose words I remember never a one.

But what I do remember in vivid detail are trivial things that had in them some touch of humour, and now I come to analyse them I see that they always concerned the under-dogs and the enemies of authority. And maybe because all my life I had been both, even if it were only Methodism that gave a faint feeling of subservience and squires and parsons in the mass who were the enemies. But I claim no monopoly of that sympathy for the under-dog, which all of us regard as a national and sporting perquisite. For Charlie Chaplin is beyond all insularity, and some of us remember that at the time of the South African War there was scarcely a nation in Europe that was not for the Boers and against ourselves.

I remember Harrison; indeed, whenever I think of the school he comes immediately to my mind. For when Tubby Mills took us in the earlier stages of German we knew the penalties for failure were drastic in the extreme, and yet Harrison would boast that he did not do homework, for he had patented a method that for effrontery and masterliness of simplicity could never have been equalled.

His seat was a front one, and so near to the table at which Tubby sat that if the two had got to their feet they could have leaned forward and shaken hands. And yet Harrison would have at the top of his desk a pile of books, including a couple of German dictionaries, and behind them would be the *open* German grammar on which we were being questioned. As the eyes of the master fell to the book to have ready the next question, so Harrison's eyes would fall to his, and by the time his turn came, he would have his answer pat. Never was he found out and never do I remember his falling below the necessary standard. What happened in written examinations is another matter.

I think that Sammy Greenhill was the most likeable boy I ever knew at Ouseland. He was a boarder, an all-round sportsman, incorrigibly lazy and possessed of the most cheerful of grins and optimisms. I recall a Cambridge Local Examination at which the supervisor was a clergyman from a neighbouring village; a man of learned looks and grimly austere. Every now and again he would look up from whatever he was reading at the head master's desk and cast round the small room a long look that should have frozen the blood of the possessor of a crib. At intervals he would stretch his legs and make a solemn promenade, casting the same terrifying looks upon us. But Sammy was quite unmoved. I, sitting almost beside him, was scared out of my wits, for on Sammy's knees was the open book and he was copying down the propositions straight from the horse's mouth. Even then he failed in the subject and because in that examination paper the riders happened far to outnumber the propositions.

But the supreme sensation of my time was the rebellion of a boy whom I will call Smith. He had a name that was famous in the school's history, and at the time of the affair was the school's fast bowler and finest footballer it probably ever had. I know he was much older than myself and that I regarded him with an enormous awe. What his offence had been I do not know, though it must have been particularly opprobrious, for one summer evening after prayers the school was told to remain at its desks, and Smith was called to the front of the school to receive a public thrashing. There was a hushed awe as he left his desk and went forward. Old Benn produced a cane from under his own desk and came round to the open space.

But an astounding thing happened.

'Stay where you are!' Smith told him fiercely.

The Head stayed, but only for a moment. Smith backed towards the arch door.

'Stay where you are!' Smith warned him again, but the Head moved on.

Then Smith suddenly whipped round and an ink-pot from one of the desks was in his hand. He held it poised. The Head halted. We gasped, and craned to watch the outcome.

For a long minute the two watched each other. Then Smith dropped the ink-pot and made for the door. He slammed it behind him and we gave another gasp. The Head, outwardly unruffled, went back to his desk and announced in his usual voice that we might dismiss. But there was never an official expulsion. I never clapped eyes on Smith again. He was a day-boy and I believe his parents left the town.

Of the trivial matters there was the affair of Wilson and the brandy-ball. In my first years W. C. Wilson—so called to distinguish him from the Burrell's works Wilsons—was my greatest friend. He was a boarder whose home was in London, and what brought us together was a mutual liking for the Stanley Weyman or cloak-and-dagger school of fiction. He would tell me about the theatre, for which he had a passion, and ultimately he became an actor. We soldiered together during the last war, and shortly after it he died at an early age when taking a leading part in a West End production.

I lost his friendship on the day Cecil Rhodes died, for Wilson saw the morning paper before me and when he informed me in hushed tones that Rhodes was dead, I said that it was about time too, or words to that effect. But Wilson had no knowledge of those Friday night rides of mine with William Cash and how through Cash's eyes I had come to regard Rhodes and Jameson as almost the equals in infamy of Joe Chamberlain himself. But to get back to the brandy-ball that Wilson happened that morning to be sucking when Tubby Mills had finished examining us in German.

Now Wilson had a peculiar nervous trick—he grew out of it in later life—of twitching his neck round so that he looked as if he were biting his own shoulder. That morning Mills was reading some book and we were at private study. Sammy Greenhill rolled a paper and chewed blotting-paper for wads and pellets and began the usual pastime of taking shots at the neck of those in front of us, and one was aimed at Wilson. But at that very moment Wilson had a nervous *tic*, and the wad went into his gullet. He choked and gasped for the brandy-ball stuck in his throat. His eyes bulged as he got to his feet. Mills rose too and surveyed the strange spectacle. Then by a supreme effort the twin impediments were at last dislodged and wad and brandy-ball were decanted on the desk.

'And what are those disgusting objects?' demanded Mills.

'Sweets, sir,' Wilson told him when he had got his breath.

There followed a monstrous imposition and then Mills was asking if any of the repulsive objects were left. Wilson handed him the packet. A minute or two of sarcasms followed and then Wilson was bidden to hand that packet round the form and to bring back any balance. But there was no balance.

But Mills did not then proceed to punish the rest of us, for eating in form, after the manner of a master named Johnson. One afternoon Johnson was going fishing and he took with him two seniors to look after the boat—Greenhill and myself. We rowed towards Brandon and came at last to where Johnson began his operations.

'Can we smoke, sir?' suddenly asked Sammy, who was getting bored.

'Certainly you can, Greenhill,' he was told, and thereupon Sammy produced to my amazement a pipe and pouch.

'I think I'd better take those,' said Johnson, and reached for them.

'But you said I could smoke, sir!' protested Sammy.

'I know I did,' said Johnson. 'In answer to your question I admitted that you could smoke. What I never said was that you might.'

Sharp practice that, and ever since that afternoon I have been a stickler for the correct use of those two words.

I admit that in the intervals of crime I must have been something of a respectable person and that the intervals themselves must have grown greater. I recall Speech Days and how I managed always to receive a prize, and there were times when I had two or three. But I should confess that they were usually for English or German. In English I had got away to a flying start, thanks to John Balfour, and was never caught, while in German I was soon to be the only senior who took that subject. But I did win an occasional form prize and one for drawing. To-day I had a look at those prizes and more than ever am I amazed at the utter lack of sympathy and understanding that was shown in their choice, for a finely tooled leather binding bearing the school crest was apparently the be-all and end-all. This is my list, though I believe one or two are missing.

Ruskin's *Seven Lamps of Architecture;* a complete *Spectator* in one volume; and an exactly similar volume for another subject! Lubbock's *Scenery of Switzerland*, which is no illustrated guide to that country but a work of geology; Lubbock's *Pleasures of Life* which were certainly not my pleasures; a volume, pages still uncut, called *The Lives of Twelve Good Men*, the twelve being obscure bishops whose names I have never seen elsewhere, and finally two volumes of Green's *Making of England*, which is tough going to-day. Had I been given a first-class dictionary or atlas or even a stack of penny dreadfuls, I should have benefited more than I did from those unhappy volumes.

As for the speeches to which we listened on Speech Day, I do not recall, as I said, a single word of any one of them. One guest of my time was Henry Lee-Warner of Tinkersham. That was in my first years at Ouseland, and I remember that while I was waiting for the Hareborough and Tinkersham train, he came up to me on the station platform and asked to see one of my prizes.

'Do you think you'll enjoy this?' he asked me.

'Yes, sir,' I said dutifully and promptly. That volume was *The Lives of Twelve Good Men*, and I can still see his dry smile. But of Henry Lee-Warner we shall hear much more later.

Towards the end of my time I was given permission to visit friends in the town on a Thursday afternoon or to spend an hour or two in the Mechanics' Institute in the market-place. The last time I was at Ouseland I went there to renew my youth, but alas! it had gone. I owe it an enormous debt. Not only did it place at my disposal reference books which the school did not possess, but it had the daily papers to put me abreast of the times, and weekly illustrateds and *Punch*, even if it was to be a good time before I considered that latter the equal of my former *Comic Cuts*.

As for games, I played for the first elevens, though better then as a footballer than a cricketer. In my last year an accident kept the captaincy from me, but later a nephew was to have that honour and of making his hundred for the school. But my best feat was at the school sports in my last year. I take no credit. Once more in my life when I was in need of advice and help, a helper appeared. Indeed he was more than a helper, for he actually forced me to become a runner.

The driver of a brewer's dray that regularly came to the village was a certain Pat Ayton, in his time a noted long-distance runner, though in my day with limbs distorted by rheumatism. It so happened that my brother was at home, and he was a good quarter-miler. I was brought in as a sprinter to accompany him on the last hundred or so yards, and it was while we were at it one evening that Ayton happened to see us. Thereafter he advised us as to our training, and he would mix oils and embrocations for us, and arrange for try-outs to synchronize with the evenings of his village calls.

But it was my speed that impressed him most. I knew I could run—I often had good reason to!—but I did not know how fast. A few years later I was only just to miss level time for the hundred, but Ayton was already seeing possibilities. He asked me why I had not run in the School Sports, and I said I stood no chance against six-footers. He laughed at me at that, and said that it would take a good big 'un to beat me. And what about hurdling?

The upshot was that I trained seriously for the sports of my penultimate year. They were held at the end of the summer term and then, unfortunately, I had a severe sprain that crippled me for months, and it was not till my last year that I had a chance to see if Ayton was right. And never was there such a fiasco. Both Burrows and Neil Wilson ran against me in the senior hundred and the farther we went the farther I drew away. As for the hurdles, my opponents jumped them as they came to them. I had been taught the whole art, and I do not exaggerate when I say that I had breasted the tape while they were clearing the last hurdle. The high jump was a walk-over for I had always been able to jump my own height, and then before I could have a shot at any other event, word went out that no competitor would be allowed to take more than three prizes. But I had a shot at the quarter-mile for all that and finished in the ruck.

My last term was all too short. I happened to be top of the school if only because the far brainier Burrows was too engrossed in his Civil Service work. But I seem to recall that I was a person of some importance to whom the Head would be gracious and with whom masters would sometimes confer. And then came the week of my final examination, and for me those days at Ouseland at last were over.

And now you may ask what it was that I got from my school. The question is pertinent for there are many things of which I have seemed to complain. But of one of them—its methods of teaching—the complaint was rather a statement of fact. And it should be remembered that fifty years ago the system of specialist teachers had not yet been devised, and when a man is Jack of all trades, there are some of which he can be nothing approaching a master.

There are things which all of us owe to all our schools: friendships, for instance, and the passport to more; what skill we have in games, and above all, innumerable memories. Those things are the heritage of all of us from all our schools, but to me they are the smallest of the debts I owe.

Perhaps I may be permitted to put it another way. It is fifty years ago. I am my father and I have a son, but to the knowledge of my father I add miraculously the knowledge that I now have. But I still send my son to Ouseland. There I know that he will have to stand on his own two legs. If there is in him anything worth the having, it will have its tests, and survival and growth will be in his own hands. In his teaching he will not be spoon-fed. When he once stands on his feet he will have to make his way forward alone. When he leaves that school he may be possessed of a self-reliance that may even make him impatient of future help. And though he may enter the school both rustic and unformed, it will be his fault if after his schooling he does not leave it with at least the making of a man.

Inadequate, perhaps, and yet it may explain why I was so puzzled when my young chance acquaintance mentioned my name as one that the school still held in good repute. Even now I can think of nothing which I ever contributed to the greater honour of Ouseland. But to say that to Ouseland I owe everything would be fulsome and untrue, and to say that

I owe it much would be an understatement. Between those two lies the truth, and in those strange urges that make me wish at times to revisit that ancient school again.

But perhaps you might like to know what happened at that final examination. There are things that you can guess—that I got distinctions in Religious Knowledge and English, and that I failed hopelessly in higher mathematics, fortunately not a main subject for me. But I also got a distinction in Geography and for once in my life I claimed the sole credit. The subject was Europe, and I devised such a comprehensive series of mnemonics that I knew every town in its place on every river and could have drawn with closed eyes the most obscure of its regions. But what we called Geography in those days was far different from the scientific and sensible subject it has become to-day.

I was awarded another scholarship that would have taken me to Cambridge. But mercifully it didn't, or I might have become an exceedingly minor don or something as staid and static and respectable as a publisher. In any case I had already left home when the news of the award came. But many things were to happen before that.

Chapter XII

CRICKET

IF the backbone of our national game is the cricket of our villages, then the backbone of village cricket is the play or sports ground of a village school. That is something in which I have always taken an interest, though an unsuspected one. What I do suspect, and at this moment, is that my voice will cry in an exceedingly lonely wilderness.

For it seems to me that in an enormous number of schools —and not only village and primary schools at that—there are three things that are radically wrong. I have never been more than a respectable amateur who made odd hundreds and took various numbers of wickets, and it may seem strange that I should raise my voice at all. But to me an English village would be shorn of much if it had no eleven, and many a village has come to that sad pass because it had never trained and interested sufficient of its village lads to ensure not only an eleven or elevens but competition for places in those teams.

Take the question of practice pitches. In my judgment a practice wicket should have the quality of a match pitch. Even one strip of matting will remove the terrors of the roughest of wickets, and yet how many urchins begin their cricket on playground and meadow corners where to stand up to a ball of any pace is to deserve more than a medal. Many a youngster has been so scared out of his wits that cricket from then on has ceased to be a game. And yet from confidence at the wicket everything must come—the use of the feet not from the ball but to it, and the watching of a ball till it meets the bat.

When I was still at school I saw a practice wicket near Lutterworth that gave me to think. The squire of the village had made a wicket of railway sleepers and matting was used on top of it. I played in a match for that village and was amazed at the standard of cricket shown—until it was all explained to me by the sight of that practice pitch. Since then I have made such pitches of sleepers or concrete, and I know that they did enormous good.

Then there is the question of the length of an initial pitch. I rarely remember to have seen the match of even the smallest of boys played on a pitch whose length was proportionate to their size. And to expect a small boy to bowl a normal cricket ball the twenty-two standard yards and find and retain length and gain something of pace, is manifestly absurd. And it is the same with gear. A heavy, full-sized bat is merely a kind of club in a small boy's hands. I have known many a men's village side that had never dreamed of possessing a couple of Harrow-sized or short-handled bats for the use of its smallest members. And yet those men would carefully select a scythe and take pains over its true balance, and at other work they would excuse an awkwardness by saying that they didn't happen to be using their own tools.

A bat is the tool of a young cricketer's craft. He must grow up with the smallest and arrive by stages at the one that finally comes readiest to his methods and hand. All my later life I have used a light-weight, short-handled bat, and it was because I happened to own such a one fifty years ago that I was able to practise what we knew as strokes. To the slogger it may be the supremest joy to clout the bowling to all parts of a field, but to the average, thinking batsman it is the making of strokes that gives the thrill. But a village batsman must be made aware in his earliest years that there are such things as strokes; call them, if you like, methods designed to counter a bowler's wiles. You may remember that I learned Euclid for months at Ouseland without even a vague idea of what it was all about, and an incredible number of young cricketers begin and end their cricket with the same absence of knowledge. There is no need to give strokes fancy names. My father, in his later years, developed what he called a nudge, but that detracted in no way from the execution of what was in reality a skilful leg glide.

And lastly there is the teaching, even rudimentary, of the art of bowling. In many villages there is only one kind of bowler whom it considers worth the name—the shut-eye slinger. The faster the pace, the better the bowler. Something of which such cricket sides remain in happy ignorance is the fate that would befall such a bowler on a fair wicket against a good bat. That a slow bowler may have some merit is grudgingly recognized, but he is always second-class. A village might read of the feats of Colin Blythe or Leveson-Gower and still be unimpressed, for a village is conservative and what is sauce for county geese may be deemed no sauce for itself.

In my young days I was considered a good bowler for I bowled a fast-medium ball. Later I took to slow off-breaks and with them I took infinitely more wickets at an infinitely less cost. And what a village side often forgets is that whereas a slow bowler—even if he cannot keep a length—has to be hit before a run is scored, a spectacular slinger is prolific in byes and every chance snick or leg touch may be a boundary. As for small boys, there is nothing that so thrills as the acquisition of a break. Once let a boy turn a ball by as little as a couple of inches, and, in my experience, he will un-grudgingly give up his leisure to the painful improving of that art. An interested bowler becomes a real bowler, for he knows that his is a craft. A village slinger is on the whole a liability to his side.

So much for the didactic. At Heathley fifty years ago we had something of a practice wicket, for the Park had a central pit that was handy for water, so we would mow a piece of ground, soak it with water and then use an agricultural roll. Fast bowling had few terrors for most of us and it was always the slow bowlers that gave us pause, for the longer a ball is in reaching you, the more time there is to get into two minds. As for sight-screens, without which and their nice adjustment even some modern village batsmen profess to be at a dis-advantage, we were unaware of their existence save on a picture of a test match in a paper in William Cash's shop.

Nor for us was the uniformity of whites. The village sides of those days were uniform only in that every man would anticipate the Sunday and don a clean shirt, and those shirts would be of various hues. Then there were the belts which some might wear: those coloured elastic belts with a snake's head fastener were the height of fashion, though many preferred the vast and spotted red handkerchief. Also most of us wore our Sunday boots, though the youngest had rubber-soled shoes, and to see a man slip up when he moved suddenly to a ball was a common enough sight. My father had shoes of his own invention—carpet slippers with a stout sole and cross straps and in the sole a number of tacks for spikes.

I have often wondered why it was that I could make runs in village cricket and yet could never make any quantity for the school, and the reason I think is that on the inferior village wickets one had to employ a different technique. There every ball was a potential shooter and the climax of a bowler's delivery was the moment when his ball hit the ground. Then one had immediately to extemporize a stroke in accordance with how that ball left the pitch, and unless one had a quick eye and flexible wrists, the strokes were snatchy and late. But on the better wickets that pause was disastrous. One watched the ball too long and too late.

When I arrived at Ouseland I was of such unimportance that I was relegated to a corner of the field for the scratchiest of games with my youngest contemporaries, and by the time I had brought myself into notice, George Mower had ceased to coach at the nets. At that time, too, we had acquired a new ground along the Bury Road, even if we had to wait till the sown grass had grown. But the laid wicket was good and before long I was watching the mid-week matches in which masters would appear. George Mower would still occasionally play and I can see his shortish trim figure and neat red beard and the way he would face a bowler with left elbow well to the fore. There was Hemsley bowling at his fastest, his long hair flopping over his eyes when a ball was hurled down. I remember Herbert Burrell playing for us and carting a ball clean out of the ground and through a bedroom window of a neighbouring house.

Sometimes the matches would be of Club and Ground standard, as when Quidenham came to play us. They had the Garniers in their resplendent I.Z. blazers, and Chapman Gaymer, and often one at least of the county pros. Such cricket was to me a revelation though too remote to make of me more than an admiring watcher. And then one day I was called before Tubby Mills.

'Is this your name in the paper, Home?'

It was the *Ouseland and Hareborough Times* in which was a report of a Heathley match in which I had happened to make a good score. Nothing else was said at the time but the following week I happened to look at the notice-board that always hung inside the school on the main archway, and there was the side to play Saham on the following Wednesday, and at the bottom of the list was my name!

I was being taken on chance for I had never appeared at anything so august as the first eleven nets. Also the Saham match was usually a walk-over, and so there was not much risk in giving a blind trial even to me. But I do remember my father's pride and fluent advice, and my mother's anxiety that my whites should be immaculate. When the day came we left Ouseland soon after lunch, and made the journey by brake and by that road that I used to cross each Wednesday of my holidays when I went with Walter Addis and Punch. I suppose we went by brake because the trains were inconvenient, but I do know that on that journey I kept myself to my insignificant corner and maybe because Old Benn himself accompanied us.

But I shall never forget that match. It was years before I was to overcome a bad attack of nerves at a wicket for the first couple of overs, but that day I was simply petrified with fear. We batted first and when my turn came to go to the wicket I was so seized with fright that I was incapable of grasping my bat. But I must have somehow moved it, if only to allow of the passage of the first straight ball, which shattered my stumps. Then when we took the field I was put at point. For the slow bowler I was moved to silly point, and I remember Old Benn on the boundary telling me to get in still closer. Maybe I did, but I know that the only sitter I had I promptly put on the floor. And when we went in to bat a second time, I secured another duck, and it was with that story that I returned home that night to my father.

But what I principally recall of those school matches are the rides in the two-horse brakes. I remember an evening when we were returning from Banham, whose head master was that Mr. Cole who, on the retirement of Old Benn, became head master of Ouseland. Never were there such teas as those at Banham. I seem to remember an infinity of cakes and dishes of various jams, though my remembrances are not entirely for that or for the fact that I for once had made some runs. As usual it is the trivial thing that comes vividly back: the sudden turning into an open heath as we were nearing home and how Greenhill and Wilson broke into a song then popular in London—*The Honeysuckle and the Bee*. I can see that lovely evening now with the sun gilding the green of the bracken and hear our voices as we sang over and over again the chorus of that song.

But the coming of the autobus and charabanc was to rob those leisurely journeys of most that was worth while. Into cricket, even village cricket, there came the feeling of haste; the haste once a match was over to get away and to some new pleasure, as if a match in retrospect were no pleasure in itself, and a stately game did not demand a stately or leisurely withdrawal. I was to see the time when a cricket match ended sharp at six-thirty because the young players were anxious not to miss the second house at a cinema in a town.

But what has made me most often impatient in these latter years has been a request to contribute towards the travelling expenses of village teams, and teams whose farthest matches lay no more than ten miles away. In my young days we walked or we cycled if there was no chance of a ride in a trap. A cricket match was an event; ample for a week rather than a day. Many a time have I cycled a dozen miles and more to a match, and that on a bicycle that would daunt a modern rider and carrying a cricket bag or some of my gear, and after a match that ended at the last possible moment I would cycle home those ten or a dozen miles as part of the match itself. Now the young men must go by motor-coach and some one else must pay for their comfort, and when it is I who am asked, I fly into a passion. I wonder now if I am right, or is it that I am merely a besotted die-hard whose head and pocket are both in the past.

In my last years at Ouseland, George Mower stood umpire for the school and as such was as fair and judicial an umpire as ever I've known. Only once do I remember his openly showing disgust and that was at the decision of a brother umpire. It was on one of those rare occasions when the school played a strong village team, and their crack batsman had tried a short run and his bails were off when he was a good two yards from the crease. The appeal was hearty and unanimous.

'Not out,' said their umpire.

'Where are your eyes?' snapped a master who was playing.

'Well, sir, I'm here to interpret the rules o' cricket,' he was pontifically told. 'What I don't see I don't give, and I happened to be lightin' my pipe.'

An old cricketer in a neighbouring village gave me as a boy one method of circumventing the malice of the opposing umpire, and I use that epithet designedly. I never saw him actually use it, nor did I have the nerve to use it myself, but I have no doubt that within its limited scope it might come in handy. A favourite method of getting a man out was an appeal for a catch behind the wicket when a ball came anywhere in the neighbourhood of the batsman's bat, or gloves or wrist. On such occasions this particular batsman would anticipate the inevitable appeal by immediately rubbing his forearm, and if there were a genuine touch he would simulate a certain agony. But if the umpire was obdurate and gave him out, then the batsman would be indignant. The rubbing of the forearm would have produced a redness, and this would be exhibited as an obvious proof of where the ball had struck, and what with that and the quoting of the cricket rule in question, the umpire might be induced to change his mind.

For my part I have been swindled out on so many and varied pretexts that I have lost count, though one of the most flagrant was when in running between the wickets I knocked a wicket down. It was no use quoting a rule, and out I had to go. But the worst example of which I was the victim was engineered by an Etonian!

When a very young man I was accustomed in my holidays to accept the request of two Etonians to bring a team to play against their estate team on the ground at the family Hall. During this particular match a strong wind was blowing; so strong in fact that one had to shout to be heard. I was batting and the elder of the sons of the house—then about sixteen—was keeping wicket, and mightily he fancied himself. A fast ball went by my bat on the off. So pleased was he at taking it that he yelled, 'How's that?'

The wind was towards the umpire and he did not raise his hand.

'You're out,' the wicket-keeper told me.

I said I had heard no decision and I walked a pace or two towards the umpire and yelled to know what his verdict had been. Before I could get an answer, the wicket-keeper whipped the bails off and appealed to the square-leg umpire, and he gave me out!

'What for?' I said. 'The ball's dead in any case.'

But out I had to go, and that was the last time I took a team to play against the N——s.

But the chief thing I remember about those matches at that Hall was the magnificence of their lunches. Never have I seen anything like them since, for there would be a butler presiding with at least two footmen in livery, and the cold dishes would include luxurious meat pies and galantines as well as most sorts of cold joints. For sweets there would be tarts and rum trifles with abundant cream, and the most amusing part of it all would be to watch the reactions of any village player whom I had taken there for the first time. But the one who most enjoyed those lunches was Squibs.

Squibs—I don't know that I ever knew his real name—was one of the best-known figures of our cricket. By trade he was a chimney-sweep, though later Lionel Robinson made him an assistant groundsman at Old Buckenham. But Squibs was also famous as a bird-watcher and every spring a letter from him would appear in the *Eastern Daily Press* announcing the arrival of this and that bird.

He was a shortish, lithe, and yet loose-limbed man with the heart of a couple of lions. For a game of cricket he would at any time have bartered his soul, and distance was no obstacle. Once he had told you he would be there, there he would be. As a batsman he was unreliable but he would bowl all day and never tire or lose heart. But it was the lovableness of the man that endeared him to every one, and when his wits gave way and he died at quite an early age in an asylum, the news cast a gloom over our cricket. But what I like to recall is the first time Squibs went to that Hall. His eyes bulged when he saw that lunch table and he looked at me as if to be assured that it wasn't a dream. But on the second occasion he merely cast an eye round as if to make sure that the anticipated feast was there, and then he gave me a flagrant wink and set to. Even the butler would smile dryly when Squibs had got seriously down to the business in hand.

But fifty years ago we had innumerable cricketers as keen as Squibs. Brackford is a hamlet that comes most readily to mind, for I doubt if the population exceeded fifty and yet I never knew them without a team. Boys and old men would be pressed into service, but play they would, and a mighty good hand they made of it. They were the only side in our district who, on account of the roughness of the only available pitch, had to use a matting wicket. Visiting bowlers would regard it dubiously and say it spoiled their run, and the mere apprehension of it would doubtless upset their delivery, for Brackford could always make runs.

But there were few keener cricketers than my father, and many a time as a small boy have I listened to my mother's upbraidings when there was work that could be done on a Saturday afternoon, or when she knew that on those mornings my father would never go far afield in case he should be too late in his return, but would often almost waste the morning by pottering in barn or fields. But whatever the urgency or the financial crisis that loomed, my father never gave way. His argument was that if a man had worked all the week he was entitled to some leisure on the Saturday, and there was the point that our cricket lasted only three months at the most. So immediately after dinner on those days he would begin his dressing, and when that was done he would be looking restlessly at the clock till it was time to take the brown paper parcel that contained his spiked shoes. Then it would be, 'Come on, son. We don't want to be late,' and off we would go to harness the horse.

But my most unforgettable cricketer would be old Arthur Sayer of Rockland. In his young days he had been batsman and bowler, but even when I first knew him he was of no value to a side except to count as one. What he was, was the Grand Impresario of cricket in Breckland and south-west Norfolk. If any Hall or house-party wanted a match, then all that was needed was to apply to Arthur Sayer, and even if Arthur had to hunt half the county, a team would be brought, and he himself would always be one.

As a registrar of births, marriages, and deaths, he had leisure for his hobby, or should I say his ruling passion, for with Arthur the year began in May and ended in late August. He was a man of fragile appearance. Even his grey beard was uncommonly thin, and when he rode abroad on his bicycle, it was hard to see if he really moved, so incredibly slow, and yet stately, was his progress. That, too, was how he bowled, for as provider and captain of his sides he would always put himself on at some stage or other of the match. Either the match was won and Arthur would announce in his thin, piping voice that it didn't matter, or if a couple were firmly set it would be that he might upset the partnership himself. Then, his grey cloth cap well on his head, he would take three or four shuffling steps to the wicket and deliver a ball in the old round-arm style, but a ball so slow that it seemed as if it could never reach the wicket. And when he batted he would announce that he never ran short runs. At a hit for one and a half he would shake his head and turn his back and begin talking to the fieldsman, and a hit for four would produce one at the rate of his slow amble. But all that was if the other batsman had struck. If Arthur himself had hit the ball—a scoop to leg was his favourite shot—then he could get between wickets as well as most.

As an impresario he was a tyrant when players were plentiful.

'I might be able to get you a place,' he would say. 'But what about you having a game next Saturday at So-an-so.'

That might be some village match, and only if the player showed good form would Arthur give him his chance in a better game. Once, as a boy, I rode miles to play for him in an all-day match, and I wanted to do well, for if I did I should be chosen for the match of the year at a certain Hall. But I had the misfortune to get a duck, and for the rest of the afternoon Arthur ignored me. But luckily we had a second innings and I made fifty. When I came out Arthur rushed up to me as if I'd been a long lost brother.

There was no practice within the law, however sharp, of which old Arthur was not capable, and when he chose a side he would be sure that on paper at least it was certain to beat the other side by an innings. You might be bringing a side against his, only to find at the last minute that he had wheedled your best men away. Or you would arrive on his ground for what you had thought a nice friendly match and find against you two or three county men whom he had brought from the ends of the earth. I remember such an occasion when we found ourselves opposed to Cant, the county fast bowler. Such speed was a revelation to us and most of our rustic batsmen were out before they were in. I know that we were slaughtered but Arthur gave no apologies. He had won and that was that.

But I also remember Arthur not only as one to whom I had to be deferential in my holidays, but as the possessor of the most unusual handshake. Yet it wasn't a handshake. When Arthur met you he would put out a hand, but his eyes would always be looking vaguely away. The hand itself was utterly limp and warm, and when you took it, it was as if one were taking something strange and unnatural and so lifeless as to be no part of the man who proferred it. Almost the last time I felt that hand Arthur was wishing me good-bye, and saying like a man in a dream that the match we had been playing was the queerest he had ever known.

Maybe it was. It was an all-day match against Donovan's Eleven at Carbrook Hall. We batted first and I happened to make some runs, and at lunch-time was still in. After lunch some players disappeared and as the afternoon wore on, others received telegrams and went too. Just as it was decided that no more substitutes could be found and that the match would have to be abandoned, I had a message too, and I said good-bye to Arthur. For that was on the August Bank Holiday of 1914.

And that brings me to four years on. In *Autumn Fields* I mentioned Bob Bennett the Heathley publican who joined up at sixty or so, and ended up driving camels in Palestine. I was behind the line and attached to another regiment shortly after my meeting with Bob near Deir Sineid, and an Indian Regiment lying near us suggested a game of cricket. They had the gear if we could provide the ground, and forthwith every available man was at work clearing a space on the hard bed of the Wadi Ghuzzeh. The wicket, and remarkably well it played, was of hard sand and earth that had been well tamped and watered.

Now our captain knew little of the capabilities of his men and it was only by chance that I, quite new to the Regiment, was asked at the last moment to make one. I did admit, on being asked, that I batted a bit and bowled a bit, but that must have been the answer of every one else. I was in at number seven and I had a very heavy bat. When at the wicket I made a flourish or two with it to see how it would suit my wrists, the crowd seemed to think I was showing off and there was a bit of a laugh and some cat-calls. But I did make twenty-nine and I know that because I have before me the cutting from the *Egyptian Gazette*.

But that is neither here nor there. After the match whom should I see but Bob Bennett.

'What are you doing here, Bob?' I said.

'Come in this mornin', m'old beauty,' he told me, and he meant that his camels had brought our chlorinated water. 'Then they reckoned as how there was a cricket match and I knew if there was any cricket you'd be a-playin', so I sorta stayed on. Didn't do so bad either.'

He explained. When I walked to the wicket he had not given away the fact that he had known me from a child, and many a time had seen me give that preliminary twirl of a bat. Then when there was a derisive laugh at my flourishing of that particular bat, he had had an idea. Bob had been a Norfolk dickey-dealer[1] and if there is anything on two legs that is more astute I have yet to meet it, and I have had dealings with many Armenians.

The ratios, I believe, are two Scotsmen to one Jew, two Jews to one Chinaman, and two Chinamen to one Armenian. I would add two Armenians to one old-time Norfolk dickey-dealer.

'Look to me as though that there young officer might be a cricketer,' he announced. 'Wouldn't mind bettin' he make a few runs.'

The bet was that I'd make double figures, and he took several bets to that effect. Until I'd passed that total he was in an agony of apprehension for the bets had amounted to a considerable sum. But I like to think that Bob wasn't betting for money, money though there was. That was only the symbol. It was in me that Bob had faith, and not somehow in me, but in the cricket he had seen and was to see again in Heathley.

[1] General dealer who travels about in a dickey (donkey) cart.

Chapter XIII

TINKERSHAM

SCHOOLDAYS, despite the assurances of parents and head masters to the contrary, are, as I remarked to the assembled scholars on a certain Speech Day, by no means the happiest of our lives. I hope that my happiest days are yet to come, but among the happiest that are gone are those I spent at Tinkersham.

Ouseland, the capital of Breckland, lies in its heart. Tinkersham lies just within its northern boundary, and if there is a lovelier town in all Norfolk I have yet to see it. But my stay there was connected with a certain examination, the passing of which was to offer me a wholly unexpected career. But that examination—the one on the journey to which I outdistanced the parson on that bicycle ride to London—required Latin to a fairly high standard, and of that language I knew no word. And then we heard that at Tinkersham Henry Lee-Warner was making a hobby of taking village and town boys in various subjects, and he willingly agreed to take me. As a famous Liberal he was known to my father.

Henry Lee-Warner comes high in my list of unforgettable men. At Rugby he had been second master under Dr. Temple, and there he had had the two Chamberlains—Austin and Neville. More than once Austin publicly spoke of the debt he owed to Lee-Warner, and I have a letter he wrote me to the same effect. I remember Lee-Warner telling me that when John Morley happened to be staying in Birmingham, Joe

Chamberlain would request Temple to let the boys be at home for that particular week-end, since a week-end in the company of Morley was a liberal education. A curious and ironical sequel, that, to those talks of William Cash on a Friday evening as we rode home from Wortley.

In his retirement at Tinkersham Lee-Warner would freely give his services to the advancement of any boy who might be in need of special coaching in any subject which he considered himself capable of teaching. I would go three times a week to his house and the intervals would be spent on the tremendous amount of homework he gave me, and chiefly from Bradley's *Latin Prose Composition*. On the first visit I paid him I expected him to be appalled at what lay before us, for in six months I had to learn the language and be capable of translating Cicero and Virgil. But when he read the syllabus he made no comment except to ask me if I was prepared to work.

The Lee-Warners were a fine old Norfolk family and of Henry it could have been said as was said of Burke that to be in his company for only a moment was to know that one had been in the presence of an intellect of the first quality and a gentleman in the supremest sense of that misused word. In appearance he was tall and somewhat frail. His lofty forehead and thinnish white beard gave him a look of austerity, but his large grey eyes held a kindly and perpetual twinkle. In my young experience he was unique and I had for him a reverent affection such as I have never since felt. His manner was quiet and urbane, and his courtesy as gentle as unforced. John Balfour, Walter Addis, Henry Lee-Warner, those were the three men to whom I owed most in life, and though I place them in that order I do not know to which of the three I owe the most. But I do know that in Elysium it is Henry Lee-Warner whom I would most like to meet.

At first I was overawed by his house and the vast extent of its grounds, but I soon came to know both well. Above all I grew to love the library where we worked, with its view to the gardens and its shelves of books to the lofty ceiling and the faint scent of their leather bindings. I can hear the rather husky voice as we went over my homework and I began translations. For the *Aeneid*, Book II, he needed no text and at the

Conticuere omnes, intentique ora tenebant

the husky voice would acquire a sonority. Cicero's *De Lege*

Manilia was less familiar but that, too, he would declaim. And when work was over for the day he would have other methods of improving my mind and outlook. Dante he loved and would make me read from the Cary's translation which he afterwards gave me. When he knew that my French was better than that of most, he would make me read Racine or Corneille, and it was he who so long ago introduced me to Trollope.

One afternoon after work he took me out to the garden. He had grown many varieties of strawberries and I was to say which of the many appealed most to my palate, and when I had given my unreliable verdict he took careful notes in his book for the benefit of his head gardener. In the months of May and June he would have each afternoon his chair brought out to the copse that lay beyond the kitchen garden, and there, the familiar umbrella as a shield against the sun, he would sit and listen to the nightingales, and, though I do not know it, I think he would read Theocritus. As for his other activities, he was a County Councillor, a magistrate, and a governor of many schools, including Ouseland, and he had stood for Parliament as a Liberal, and it is strange how to me that list comes as an anti-climax.

But there were other rough edges of mine of which he must have been aware, for he would make me stay to tea when there were even distinguished guests, and on at least two occasions I went to dinner. At one there was present that same bishop who had presented the prizes at Ouseland, and I know that Henry Lee-Warner spoke kindly of me when he presented me to the great man. As for his courtesy I give just one example.

It happened that my father and Peacock had business at Tinkersham for the Oddfellows' Club, and so much did I revere Henry Lee-Warner that I insisted on taking them round to see the great man. I obtained leave so to bring them and I know now that the time was an awkward one—just before dinner, in fact—but he suggested no alteration. In the library the three talked, and chiefly about Liberalism, and when my father rose at last to go he was so impressed by the character of the man that he expressed what he felt in the only way he knew.

'Thank you for having us here, sir,' he said, 'and thank you for what you're doing for my son. And if you're ever round Heathley way, sir, don't you ever dare go through without dropping in for a cup of tea or something.'

Lee-Warner thanked him and assured him that he would, and if he had ever come as far as Heathley I know he would have at least looked my father up. But when my mother heard of that invitation she was horrified.

'Just fancy,' she said. 'A gentleman like that coming into this little house for tea!'

'I don't know for that?' said my father angrily. 'He's a gentleman, ain't he? And he's a Liberal, like me.' And after a snort he added his usual, 'Well, then!'

One afternoon when I went to the house as usual, I was told that there was a matter to discuss. Those were the first days of the No Hat Brigade as it was called, and I had joined the movement. And why, Lee-Warner asked. I said it seemed more natural to wear no hat in the country. He began quietly pointing out the folly in life of making oneself conspicuous in anything. In that ten minutes' talk he touched on most things in which my tastes might err—dress, neckties, note-paper and the very mannerisms that made personality. The same evening I went back to a hat and it was years before I dared in my mind to abandon it.

Then there was the occasion when he said it had come to his ears that I sometimes played billiards at the George with Burras, a master from the grammar school. I admitted it, and he asked me to state a case. I put up some feeble defence which he countered by asking if work were not more important than play. I ventured to ask him if I had ever failed to give him satisfaction in my work.

He leaned back in his chair and stroked his thin beard, and I waited. Then he said, not grudgingly, that I had not, and that my leisure was my own. But he said he would have a word with Burras, and I believe he did, for after that we played but rarely. And finally, when everything was over and I was ready for that examination, he did not send me away with endless advice. He refused by his very manner to admit that the examination would be hard, and I know that gave me an unusual confidence.

Then came the day when I cycled over to see him and to tell him the examination result.

'I knew you could do it,' he said.

'Not me, sir, but you.'

I had at least the courtesy and the gratitude for that. He merely patted my shoulder and I can still see his dry smile.

For years after that he would write to me. Throughout the World War his letters would reach me in distant places and it was always a joy to see that minute handwriting, more small and crabbed and illegible as the years went by. The very last words he wrote to me were these.

> The Paddocks,
> Tinkersham,
> *May 11th*, 1918
>
> . . . I see no one these days. Neither trap nor car is good for me and railways are prohibited. Moreover I suffer from the heat of the sun on my face so that I lurk at home till the sunset when I sally forth to enjoy the gentians and the daphnes and the hyacinths. Why, then, should I grumble about my foolish and senile self when the world has such lovely things.
>
> But what a joy it will be when at last we have a talk!
> Yours ever,
> H. LEE-WARNER.

That is why I long for that talk in Elysium, even though he will be impatient of my gratitude and will turn his ear towards the nightingales.

At Tinkersham I lodged with a Mrs. Nash, who lived in a cul-de-sac lane that runs by the railway, and is known as Providence Terrace. For my board and lodging, including a tiny study of my own, I paid thirteen shillings a week, and I remember that my puddings were always cold tapioca ones eaten with stewed rhubarb which I would bring from home at week-ends

Mrs. Nash was a quaint and lovable character whom Henry Lee-Warner had strongly recommended to me. Her father had been Lord Mayor of Norwich, but her husband left so little money that she herself had barely enough on which to live. She must have been well over seventy, and a more dainty or bird-like figure I have never seen. She would talk with me in the French she had learned at her finishing school, and her voice was like the tinkle of a lovely bell. I would love now to see again her drawing-room, for she had refused to sell what remained to her of the family treasures, and that room was crammed with china and pottery, and the walls were so covered with samplers, pictures on glass, silhouettes and miniatures and gaily decorated plates that a fly must have found it hard to find a settling place on a speck of empty wall.

She, too, had a charming old-fashioned courtesy, and my heart goes out to her if only because she treated me as an equal. But she suffered from two strange delusions—that her singing voice was what it might have been in her earlier years, and that she could still play the piano. When there were guests for tea, and many of the gentry in the neighbourhood would call on her—she would sing to them and accompany herself on the ancient piano and often of an evening I would be called to the drawing-room to be entertained alone. At first I thought the piano was badly out of tune, and only slowly did it dawn on me what was wrong, for though her eyes might read the notes on the music before her, her fingers moved unconnectedly and of their own accord. But happily she always played softly and the dreadful discords could only just be heard against the cracked and wavering voice.

But there were other characters at Tinkersham who were to influence my young life. Burras of the grammar school I have mentioned, and he was also a first-class naturalist. Often of evenings we would roam the heaths and brecks in search of rare birds, and he would amaze me by identifying a bird solely by its note. It was he who first showed me the larder of a red-backed shrike, and that same afternoon we found the nest of a whin-chat, a bird I had never known. It was Burras who asked me to place in a naturalist's order of merit the hedges, ground, and trees. I, who had never nested except in hedges and ponds plumped for hedges as the best place in which to find nests. But those came last, he said. Trees came first and then the ground.

Burras had a colleague named Marks and it was with him that I spent most of my leisure, for he was a musician and an artist who had studied in Paris. Often of an evening I would blow the organ for him at the fine old parish church, and once he let me play, though all I could manage was a hymn tune, and that without the pedals. But in his room was a fine piano of his own and on it he would play by the hour. It was Marks who introduced me to the sonatas of Beethoven, though it was Chopin and his minor melancholies that were most to my ear.

Marks would spend much time at water-colour painting in the country round Tinkersham and especially on the heaths.

Well do I remember the hot afternoon when he drew my attention to what he called some fine distant blue. What he meant I did not know until through his eyes I learned to see the things that had always been there for me to see, and which my untrained eyes had missed. Soon I was looking for distant blue, and I would use a spare paint-box of his, and when he was painting I would be at an attempt of my own. From him I learned the elements of the art, and soon our house had specimens of my work. What I thought was my best effort to date I gave to my eldest sister. She said it was lovely, but wondered what a pig was doing floating about in the sky. I snatched the picture annoyedly from her hand for that pig was one of my clouds!

One day I went to sketch on the Plains. I tried to make a study of the gorse, with sage green and yellow ochre as the keys of the colour scheme. Just as I had finished, the Reverend came up to me, for he had been practising golf shots in the open spaces. I remember that he was very impressed and drew out of me who my teacher had been. And perhaps it was his appreciation that led me to make a suggestion to Fred Fox.

Fred wanted a back-cloth for his studio photographs and had no idea where to buy one. I said I would paint one myself if he would draw a rough design of what he required. Those were the days of faked stone terraces and rustic seats but we hit upon something different—a mountain in the background, a drooping tree in the middle distance and a rockery in the foreground. As colours would come out falsely I worked in blues that ranged from ultramarine to a near white, and as the canvas was immense, I had to use a house-painter's brush. Hundreds of village swains and maidens must have posed against that dreadful background, and when once I saw it in later years I went hurriedly away.

But to get back to Tinkersham and Marks. When Burras came round of an evening to his rooms, the atmosphere would create for me that little I had read of Bohemia and the Latin Quarter. There would be Marks himself with his squat Parisian figure and his hair *en brosse*, the walls with their nudes and studies in oil, the tables covered with odd music and the paraphernalia of the painter's craft and the corners crowded with frames and easels and a lay figure. There were the mugs of beer the two would drink, and Marks would play to us or we would sing student songs to his accompaniment. It is good even now to think of those nights again, even if, like the traveller of *Le Carnet du Bal*, I was to find in Paris later that few things are so far from harsh reality as the impressions of youth.

Of those young memories and impressions there is one that I often strangely recall. It was a spiritual experience, vivid and curiously lasting, the impact of which it is impossible to convey. It is of a cottage, backed by giant elms, that stands in a quiet lane in that last village before one reaches Tinkersham from Hareborough. There was the luminous glow that pervades the sky in that hour before dusk on a perfect evening of summer, and as soon as I saw that cottage I knew somehow that only in it could I do the things I wished to do and be the things I vaguely wished to be. And every time I cycled by it, whatever the hour or the weather, that feeling persisted.

Years later and in places enormously remote I would think of that cottage, and I could still feel the vision and the gleam and I would wonder what strange affinity of time and mood and circumstance had made that cottage an anchorage against unrest and a sure abiding place for body and spirit. Then years after that I came that way again. As I neared that cottage I could feel much of what I had felt on that evening of thirty years before and I tried to analyse the youth I had been. But there was no analysis of a distant self that could even begin to explain. I had had no eremitic urge; there were no pangs of despised love or surge of adolescence or a poet's wonder. What, then, had been the source of that revelation or realization—call it what you will—that I could still faintly feel?

Then at last I came to the familiar bend and I drew the car up. There was the cottage, snug beneath the elms, but to me it was something I had never seen. The visionary gleam had gone and it was never to return except in the memory of a distant summer night.

To Marks I owed an incredible deal, for it was he who opened my eyes. Like Bartimaeus I began to see, even if at first it was men as trees walking. But there were other men in Tinkersham who were to influence me. Of the last of them, an antique dealer, I shall tell you later, but meanwhile there is Canon Smith.

Granville Smith—I think that was his name—was a short, active man, spry even in his gestures and movements and with a puckish sense of humour. I think he must have been nearing seventy when I first saw him, but the white beard may have deceived me. But as soon as he knew I was something of a cricketer he told me that he was probably the only living man who had been able to bowl a shooter at will!

I have heard him announce the fact many times, and when his hearer silently debated that astounding statement and thereby showed a doubt, he would at once fetch an ancient Wisden and open it at a folded page whereon was his name. And there in black and white was written that Granville Smith—a Blue in that far-off year—had definitely the gift of bowling a shooter whenever he so pleased. But when I as a bowler asked him for the secret of that amazing gift, he would say that it had long left him. He himself had tried to recapture it, and failed, and it had gone as irrevocably as a forgotten dream. When I persisted—for such a gift or acquired art would revolutionize my cricket—he tried with sundry twists and shapings of his fingers to remember what it was that he had done, only to shake his head and confess that it was of no use.

The Vicarage faced the cricket ground and that spring the pitch was rolled with an exceedingly heavy roller that he provided. At his invitation a score or so of young men attended that evening and when the rolling was over he called them as usual to the house. There he brought out a box of cigars and handed them round as a kind of reward for effort, and then the men departed. I and the captain, a man of higher social standing than the rest, remained for some business or other. The Canon surveyed the cigar box and then put it back in the cupboard.

'Ah, well!' he said resignedly. 'It's lasted two rollings and it may do one more.'

And then he produced a box of what must have been real cigars. He passed it to the captain and me and took one himself and lighted it, and then he chuckled. It was an impish chuckle; the chuckle of a boy, who has successfully achieved some mischief; the same chuckle that had come fifty years before perhaps when he had bowled one of those devastating shooters.

But I chiefly remember the Canon and the Vicarage because

of its billiard table. It was a three-quarter size, and on two nights a week, all the year round, he would keep open house. Any one in the town who could play billiards was free to come on a first visit, and after that there would be rosters made to avoid undue crowding.

I was asked at least once a week. At eight o'clock promptly I would arrive and then there would be ceremonial coffee brought in by a maid, and after that we would play. I was no performer but that was no drawback to enjoyment, and as time went on one learned. It was amazing, too, the varieties of people that one met. Sir Arthur Wilson, the famous Sea Lord, was often there when living in his native town, and I remember a four-handed game consisting of Sir Arthur, the Canon, a young agricultural labourer and myself.

Many years after that I laid down a bowling-green in my Heathley gardens. It was less for myself than for the village, and an invitation was duly issued. No matter what his trade or religion or politics or means any man might play. All that was asked of him was that he should love the game and play it. But what the village did not know was that I was not the host or the provider of those means to enjoy a pleasant summer evening. It was Canon Smith who made that green, and on the timber front of its reed-thatched summer-house there should have been an acknowledgment of all that I owed him myself, and all that that bowling-green could never repay.

Chapter XIV

ANTIQUES

IN Tinkersham I first entered an antique shop and there I first made the acquaintance of an antique dealer. All my life I was to love those shops and whenever I enter a town I still make their whereabouts my first inquiry. Expert though I may be in some trivial things, I envy the vast and intuitional knowledge of the dealers and wish that I had somehow acquired it. But most antique dealers are gently spoken, courteous men who love the things they must sell and never urge me to buy. What they love above everything is to talk about this piece and that, and to ask opinions on something of which they are none too sure. In nineteen cases out of twenty I leave their shops without making even a small purchase, and rarely do they fail to say they will be glad to see me again.

But about that asking of opinions, even a dealer of experience may make mistakes. When I was a very young man a dealer asked my opinion of a certain china figure and particularly its age. It was of fine quality and I had a shot at valuing it. But I put the date far later than his estimate and principally on account of the clothes. It was a figure of a Dandy, by the conspicuous fur cloak and side-whiskers.

He was sure of the age but I could not agree. Then I thought of something and we consulted an encyclopedia. The whiskers were dundrearies, so named from Sothern's creation of Lord Dundreary and there then was the date, which happened to be roughly my own. That dealer was profuse in his thanks, and he presented me with a Toby snuff-taker that I had fancied.

But I had been somewhat familiar with antiques from my arrival at Heathley, for my mother had some fine quality Wedgwood plates and cups from the service owned by the aunt who brought me up. When that aunt died I came into possession of the remains of that large service. It had been a double one, but all that reached me were four coffee-cups, two cups and saucers, a sugar-basin and a broken teapot, for when my aunt had returned to London she had taken to cats, and those animals would be given their food on the plates and saucers of that exquisite service.

We also had a Bible box, the carvings of which, especially the Tudor roses, was as ornate and yet as delightful as any that I've seen. But my mother once wanted that box for a special purpose and my Uncle Ted, then on a visit to us, painted it a vivid red to suit that purpose, and neither he nor my mother had much idea of its value. Later I begged for that box, and when it was given me I removed the paint with caustic soda, but even then the wood was a reddish hue that took all value from the box itself. Later I parted with it to a dealer for a pound, and at once reinvested the money, and thereby will hang another tale.

In my young days that passion for painting would ruin the artistic and monetary values of many a fine old piece. I have a superb early Georgian cupboard and when I first clapped eyes on it in a farm-house corner, it was painted a butcher blue. Even the lovely shaped shelves were so painted, and though I had it cleaned by an expert, a sheen of blue still catches the eye in certain lights. Corner cupboards too, were always covered at their sides with the wall-paper of the room, and from one or two I have removed a dozen layers or so, with the bottom layer that of the period when the cupboard was made.

In my mother's bedroom was a chest of drawers of which no one knew the value. It was thought to be painted deal, though I own I never examined it closely. The paint, I remember, was a bright brown and varnished. Then just after the last war when prices were high and that chest no longer wanted, it was put in a sale to make what it might. I was not in England at the time, but that chest was oak and it made almost as many pounds as the shillings that had been anticipated.

When I was a very small boy and Colonel Pewtrance came to Brackford Hall and spent a fortune in restoring that marvellous Tudor House, he was anxious to furnish it with anything of the period, and he commissioned my father to buy every piece of antique oak on which he could lay his hands. As my father was no great judge and would have as guide only the age known by himself or as given from the family history, Pewtrance guaranteed him against loss. In fact he undertook to take everything that was sent to him, both good and bad. What I remember of such things was a chest of drawers, black with grime and grease, that was brought to our barn after the death of Martha *alias* Pat Bunnett, who must have been at least a hundred when she died. I see it now as very early Tudor, and probably Henry the Eighth. The feet had gone but it was otherwise in good order. What my father paid Martha's heirs, if any, I do not know, but I remember that he chuckled when Pewtrance gave him three pounds.

It will be a poor time in life when there are not tales that will hold us as children from our games and as old men from the chimney corner. I would listen by the hour to the tales that Tinkersham antique dealer would tell me.

There was the way he first began. Like many another dealer he had been a dickey-dealer as a young man, and had found the profit in furniture and oddments of china, and had abandoned general dealing for antiques. One of his first customers had advised him to read certain books, and from those and hard experience he had gradually learned his trade, though at first his simple principles had been merely to sell for more than he gave.

But his shop was small and out-of-the-way and lack of capital kept him from taking better and more commodious premises. Then came a day when he had been tramping the countryside in search of antiques while his young wife stayed at the shop. He had found nothing of much consequence, and then towards evening he saw a cottage across a meadow and he debated with himself if he should call at it or not.

'Never worry about downstairs,' was the advice he gave me. 'Any dealer can stand at an open door and see what there is downstairs. Upstairs, that's the place to look. That's where there may be a fine old chest or chair.'

He knocked at the door of that cottage and a woman opened

it. What he asked was if she could anyhow make him a cup of tea, and while she was getting it he cast his eyes around, but there was nothing worth his buying. Over the tea they got into talk and she asked him if he would lend her a hand with moving a piece of furniture from one bedroom to another. Then in one of those bedrooms he saw the chair!

It was a Chippendale chair, and just as illustrated in one of his books, and the finest on which his eyes were ever to rest. And he was able to buy it, for he offered the woman no less a sum than two pounds. That night he could hardly sleep, and in the morning he set off to London in the train, for there lived a gentleman who had asked him urgently to report any fine quality Chippendale that he should ever acquire. That customer was Holloway, of Holloway's Pills and Ointment, and his offer for the chair—an offer that was accepted—was a hundred and fifty pounds! What that chair would be worth now I do not know, but I am talking of at least eighty years ago.

One day that dealer had a bargain that was to teach him a lesson that changed his life and his business methods. Once more he was out in his pony-cart combing the distant country-side and again he had bought nothing of any particular value for his now much larger shop. Then as he drew near home, he happened to drive by a farm-house and in the barn he saw men stacking corn-sacks on a large table. That table was of no interest but he knew that discarded and unfashionable furniture could often be found in old barns, so he went across for a look round. But nothing was there and he had another look at the table.

He saw that it was massive and old and carved on it was an early sixteenth-century date. But it was far too massive to put on his cart and so large that it would scarcely get into his biggest room, so he debated with himself about trying to buy it. Then he did buy it, and perhaps because he hired a wagon from the farmer to carry it to the shop.

The table was cleaned and polished at once, and just as the work was done, who should enter the shop but the then head master of Gresham's, Holt. He was going almost at once to the Continent on a longish holiday, but as soon as he clapped eyes on that table he offered to buy it.

'To tell you the truth, sir,' the dealer said. 'I don't know what to ask you. I've never seen one like it before. not even in the books.'

He was offered twenty pounds for it and he took it. At least he accepted the offer though no money passed, for his customer said he would send for the table and give the cheque on his return, and meanwhile, might the table be stored for him. But a day or two later a London dealer happened to call in the course of his usual country rounds. He saw that table and offered thirty and then forty pounds. He was told that it was sold. A few days later came an offer in writing of fifty pounds for the table.

The dealer thought it over and he was tempted to sell. No money had passed and there was no agreement in writing, and he could reasonably claim that the original offer was grossly below the table's value. But his wife dissuaded him and the table duly made its way to Holt. Some months later the purchaser again entered the shop.

'How did you like the table, sir?' he was asked.

The answer was that the table was unique, for it was Henry the Eighth, and dated, and a perfect specimen in superb order. Then the dealer told him what had happened during that holiday.

'You're an honest man,' he was told. 'I shan't give you a penny-piece more than we agreed on, for a bargain's a bargain. But I'll see that you don't lose.'

And he didn't lose. That customer became an even better one. In his time he bought hundreds of pounds worth of articles and he recommended an honest man to all his friends.

But all dealers were not so honest. Even in those far-off days there were fakers and fakes. An old dealer—he would be a hundred and ten if he were alive to-day—told me that in his youth there flourished a firm of fakers at Ipswich, and it was they who made a certain table.

'Boy, I know the very chatch[1] from which the timber came for that there table,' old Shuck told me in his broad Suffolk. 'I know the man what made it and the blacksmith what made the nails in it and the pond they was put in to rust. And the woman what had it in her back-yard and was paid to holl[2] all the household slops and stuff all over it. And I know the man what carved the date on it, and how they used to knock it about with hammers and what not and make marks all over it.'

[1] Church.   [2] Hurl or throw.

That table was bought by the editor of a famous paper, and he afterwards told the dealer from whom he bought it that—in Shuck's own words—he wouldn't part with it, not for as many gold sovereigns as would cover the top.

Shuck, dead and gone these many years, told me a story of his own early days as a dealer that struck me as the most ingenious of the many stories of antique dealers that I ever heard. He had bought a set of chairs that had been standing for a long time in some damp attic or cellar and had consequently lost their polish. The set of chairs—six small and two carvers—would be valuable if only he could get them back to their original condition, but it was a job that he was incapable of doing himself. Then inquiries among fellow dealers brought the information that a certain Frenchman in London was the best man for the job. Shuck got into touch with him and a bargain was struck. The price paid for the Frenchman's services was very large—the colossal sum for those days of five pounds a week.

Moreover the Frenchman insisted on having a room to himself and the chairs, for he was chary of disclosing the secrets of his trade. And Shuck wasn't going to pay any man five pounds a week and see only the finished article for his money. Also if he could learn the Frenchman's secrets, he could in future dispense with his services, and do such jobs himself. So he tried every wile and strategem to get into that room, and without avail. The Frenchman was as wily as himself. When Shuck knocked at the door and tried excuses to enter, the Frenchman, though he spoke a fair English, would begin talking voluble French and keep the door merely ajar till it could be finally closed again. Shuck—and a craftier rascal even in his old age I never met—tried every trick and dodge, but the Frenchman countered every wile.

But time was going on and the job was almost finished. And then Shuck had an idea. The stairs that wound upwards past the room where the Frenchman worked were narrow and in the rooms and attics above was kept much of the stock. On those facts Shuck built his scheme, and he confided in his two men so that the scheme would be worked out. Then the hour came.

Shuck and the two men went up the narrow winding stairs to a higher room and there the two men picked up a heavy table and began to manipulate their way down. Shuck came behind. There was much struggling and cursing, and then just as the front of that table was being manipulated past the Frenchman's door, the man in front was artistically wedged against the wall and at once he began to yell at the top of his lungs. The key turned in the Frenchman's door and out his head came.

Shuck hollered to him and gesticulated. The man was hurt and if the Frenchman didn't lend a hand, the table would be smashed.

'Clar a holt[1] on't,' yelled Shuck and the Frenchman must have gathered what he meant for he did collar hold. Then the man at the far end of that table manœuvred him on, and down the stairs the table and the Frenchman went, and the Frenchman was virtually imprisoned till the ground floor was at last reached.

Shuck let the table go on and nipped into the Frenchman's room. On one of the chairs were his polishing cloths. On the floor was the little black bag which he would bring with him of a morning and into which Shuck had never been able to look. Now he did look. And instead of the foreign concoctions and oils and polishes that he expected, what should be there but only another cloth or two and a partly used tin of ordinary brown boot polish.

It was Shuck, too, who told me the story of some other chairs, and I rather fancy he had been concerned in that affair himself, for he made no bones about glorifying in his earlier rogueries. That particular set of chairs had been sold to a nobleman who made a hobby of collecting chairs of that period and he was recognized as the great authority. The price paid was—shall we say?—four hundred pounds.

But the new owner of those chairs was none too certain about them even though they had been sold with a full guarantee and description. Finally he decided that the chairs were clever fakes and he called in another expert who verified the fact. Along he went to the dealer in a fine rage. The dealer expressed amazement. He was sure the chairs were genuine but nevertheless he'd abide by his lordship's verdict. And certainly the chairs should be taken back, and his lordship should be recompensed for any expense and inconvenience. So a cheque was handed over and his lordship signed a receipt for five hundred guineas for a set of chairs.

Into that shop there came one day an American collector,

---

[1] Collar hold.

and he was shown those chairs which he was told had been specially reserved for him. The price asked was a stiff one— nine hundred guineas.

'You'll guarantee absolutely that they're genuine?'

The dealer drew the American aside, and whispered. Not a word must ever get abroad but those chairs had been bought from Lord X!

The eyes of the American bulged at the mention of that name, and he asked if his lordship was in financial straits. The dealer gave a non-committal shrug of the shoulders, and then from his pocket he produced the receipt for their purchase. Might that be included in the sale of the chairs, the American asked. The dealer said that provided discretion was used, then it might be so included. The chairs went to America.

I have said that on a certain famous day I came into the possession of a sovereign of my very own, and at once I announced my ambitious intention of starting an antique collection. It was my father who was in favour, for he knew from his experiences with Colonel Pewtrance there was money in antiques and his idea was doubtless that I wanted to buy in order to sell again.

'Why don't you go and see old George Rewell?' he said.

George Rewell was brother to that Rewell who had farmed Cranberry and to Aaron who had fallen downstairs and broken his neck on a certain Saturday when my sister and I had been gathering bullaces in his garden. George had become something of a hermit in his little holding on the edge of the Brackford brook. All the Rewells had been Methodists and my father had often asked George to kill his pigs. It was then that he would drink a glass of George's mead, and own that when driving home he could hardly see the road.

'All you've got to do,' my father said, 'is tell George whose son you are. Mind you don't go and rile him, because he's got a bit queer.'

So I walked the mile to Brackford and mightily nervous I was. George was living alone but for an aged housekeeper who was as dirty as himself. Anna Dolly was the name by which she was known; a short, enormously fat woman who suffered from asthma and wheezed and groaned at each step she took.

But as I drew near the house I had a stroke of luck. George

Rewell, shaggy-bearded and with thick overhanging eyebrows, glared at me from the bridge across the brook.

'Morning, Mr. Rewell,' I said. 'You remember me, don't
you?'

He didn't, but he knew the name well enough. I rein-
forced it with my father's name, and at once he was asking
after him. By then we were moving towards the house. The
garden was like a wilderness and everywhere hedges were
gapped. Hens were scratching in what had once been a
flower-garden along the path to the front gate. When we
came to the kitchen, the door of which stood wide open, an
indescribable scene met my eye. That brick floor had a layer
of chicken dung and dung was on the chairs and tables where
they had perched. Cobwebs hung from a superb Jacobean
corner cupboard, and on the dung of the floor a fine Mason's
dish held some filthy milk for George's cat. But two chairs
caught my eye. They were cottage Chippendale, and even
now they are worth no more than three or four pounds each,
but a beginning had to be made somewhere. Under the
chicken dung were the original rush seats.

'It's a pity to let two chairs like that get dirty, Mr. Rewell,'
I said. 'Will you sell them to me?'

'What'll you give me for 'em?' he was asking me at once.

'You're the seller,' I said. 'You tell me what you want.'

He gave me a crafty look.

'Half a crown a-piece, hurt ye?'

I frowned in thought and he watched me anxiously.

'Well, it's a lot of money,' I said. 'But I'll give it to you.'

'Give us your money,' he said, and his hand went out.

I went boldly on to the living-room. That was reasonably
clean, and above my head I could hear the wheezing of old
Anna Dolly in one of the bedrooms. On the mantelpiece
a lovely blue Spode cottage.

'I'd like to buy that cottage, Mr. Rewell,' I said, 'What
will you take for it?'

The crafty look came into his face again.

'You'll hatta give me big money for that. Adcock o'
Hareborough'—that was an itinerant watchmaker—'he bid
me big money.'

I wasn't going to miss that cottage even if it took my
remaining fifteen shillings.

'Well, Mr. Rewell, whatever he bid you, I can bid,' I said.

'Then dust ye give me half a crown?'

'That's a lot of money,' I said again. 'But I'll give it all the same.'

Out went his hand and into my pocket went that cottage. And then I gave him a shilling each for two brass pestles and mortars, and then who should come wheezing down the stairs but Anna Dolly. I asked if there was anything else I could buy.

'Show you him that there picture, Anna,' Rewell said, and Anna wheezed her way up the narrow stairs again. When she came wheezing back she was carrying a portrait in oils in a gilt frame. It was of a lady in a mauve dress with a deep lace collar. I can see it now as I write.

'They reckon that's one o' them Poleys what used to live in Heathley,' Old George said. 'One on 'em give it to my mother who used to be housemaid there. Dust you give me a crown for 't?'

The look was even craftier for George had raised his price. I would have given many times that for so lovely a portrait of one of my ancestors, but with a show of regret I handed over the two half-crowns. Then I said a temporary good-bye to George Rewell and I fairly ran back to Heathley and got the pony into the cart. We went back at full speed for fear George should change his mind. But he hadn't changed it. He actually wanted to know what I'd give for that Jacobean corner cupboard. It was in none too good a condition so I bid him ten shillings. Where I was to raise that sum I had no idea.

'Darn! no you don't,' George said. 'You'll hatta give me a pound.'

But that was beyond me, and that cupboard stood there for a few more years. Then when I had the money I asked my father to buy it, and he did. I thought restoring would spoil it so I sold it to a collector whom I knew who bid me ten pounds.

When I reached home with my possessions my father was inclined to scoff. Why hadn't I bought that oak bed that George slept on? He described the carved back to me and years later I was to see it in the house of a friend who had bought it at George's death. But I was well pleased with that first effort at collecting. For fourteen shillings and sixpence I had bought two chairs, that were, when cleaned and polished, a credit to any room, a pottery cottage in perfect order and

saleable at once for a pound, the two pestles with which my
mother was pleased, and that lovely portrait that looked even
lovelier when it had been cleaned.

A word may be necessary about the ethics of collecting. A
pompous phrase but you may gather what I mean. I had
heard in the Tinkersham shop the patter of the trade and I
had been told the art of buying. I had used it that day at
George Rewell's, but was I fair and honourable to buy for a
shilling what was worth ten? I think so, and, as they say in
Norfolk, I will tell you for why.

If when I had bought those chairs I had paid Rewell more
than he had asked, then I should have excited his cupidity and
he would have demanded impossible prices, far beyond their
worth, for other things. Many a dealer has made the mistake
of making too generous an offer, only to be told 'If you can
bid me so-and-so it's worth that to me.'

Many a time when I've made a man or woman an offer I've
said this, and meant it: 'That's all I can give you and that's the
fair value. A dealer may come along and tell you it's worth less.
When you won't sell it to him, he'll say you're wise because
it's worth far more even than I offered, only he doesn't
happen to want it. He'll do that so that you shouldn't sell
it to any other dealer.'

If it was china or pottery I would beg the woman not to
leave it exposed but to put it somewhere where it could be
seen and yet be in no danger.

'If I buy it,' I would say, 'I shall put it in a glass case and
you can come at any time and see it.'

But often one would go back and that fragile and beautiful
object would be chipped or cracked from a fall, or it would
even be destroyed. Those who do not wish to sell should
at least preserve.

Only a few years after that morning at George Rewell's,
when I had money in my pocket, I was being driven to Attley
Station. At Snettley I drew near a cottage from which a cart
was just driving away. A woman stood at the door, a handkerchief to her eyes. I had the trap stopped and got out.

'What's the matter, Mrs. Saunders?' I asked her.

She had been in monetary difficulties, she told me, and had
sent for a dealer to sell him a gate-legged table and a grandfather clock. But he had just offered only ten shillings for

the table and a pound for the clock. I had a look at them. The table was a nice one but the clock was an ordinary kitchen one with a white face.

'Suppose I give you double the amount myself?' I asked her, and her face lighted. I gave her the three pounds and ten shillings more on some pretext and told the man to collect them on his way home. But my point is that I was no philanthropist in spite of that. I bought at a reasonable price for those days. As for the dealer, he was not only a rogue but a fool into the bargain.

Except when I have bought what for me were fairly important pieces, they were always from dealers or at sales. Those pieces were bought for a definite purpose in a house, but most of my collecting has been done for a far different reason. What I came to want was a collection of antiques, however humble, that had been owned by people I knew as a boy. Those are for me the true adornments of my house and for them I was prepared to pay sums far beyond their value, though I rarely did.

There is a Queen Anne table that belonged to Walter Addis; an exquisite carved hutch that was George Spline's; a pair of candlesticks that were Wyatt's, a pottery dog that belonged to the wife of Dodger Lake, and a Rockingham figure that belonged to Shadrach Ward who used to harness old Punch. I could fill a page or two with those belongings. But I must add a chair that belonged to old Fox, the parish rate-collector at the time of the affair of the Pump.

It so happened on a certain Christmas that my house would not hold all the family and guests. For one guest—a celebrated cricketer—I found a bedroom with old Mrs. Fox, and I went to inspect it. There I saw the legs of a chair. I repeat —the legs only for the whole chair was swathed in red baize that had been fastened to it with tacks. Of the legs I could see only an inch or so above the feet. So I chanced my guess at what lay under the baize and asked what price would be taken for the chair. Thirty shillings, I was told, and so promptly that I guessed a dealer had seen it at some time or other and had offered a pound.

I bought it and carried it home, heavy as it was. When I set it down on the billiard-room table, my mother was horrified at what I had done, and when I began ripping off the baize and generations of dust flew about the room, she thought

I was mad. But at last I saw what lay beneath—a William and Mary armchair as the feet indicated. The original rush back was intact but the rush seat had been removed and a hole cut to make it a commode chair. The lovely old walnut was full of tacks but the superb arms and the turned stretcher were unharmed. When an expert had finished its restoration, even my mother could welcome yet another chair to an over-crowded house.

Of old George Rewell there is a last tale to tell. Whatever my assurances you will scarcely believe it, so I tell it as I know it.

I had often heard from my father of a day when he was at George's farm killing a pig. An old gypsy woman came to the house and when George caught sight of her she was drawing herself a bucket of cool water from his well, for it was a hot afternoon. George hated gypsies as many others did, and threatened her with his stick, and drove her away. At the gate she cursed him for denying an old woman a drop of water.

'Water will be the death of you!' is what she screeched at him, and I remember how my father would laugh when in latter years George became fuddle-witted and very much of a hermit, and water never touched his face or body.

But mark the ending, and there must be many living who will know its truth. George's house got so unutterably filthy, as did he himself, that at last it was decided that he should be taken to the workhouse infirmary. He had to be dragged protestingly to the cart, but go there he did. When the master saw his condition and smelt the stench of him, he ordered him to be bathed at once. In that bathroom George kicked and struggled with all his senile strength.. But the shock of that bath and his struggles brought on a stroke while he was in the bath itself, and that same night he died.

Postscript.

I mentioned in a previous postscript that last year I went through Heathley on my way to Tinkersham, for some urge had driven me to see again that little town. Having secured a room at the George—where once I played billiards with Burras—I made my way to The Paddocks. Two of Henry Lee-Warner's nieces had inherited the property and they were delighted to let me sit again in the room in which he and I had worked. By a strange coincidence one of them was reading my last novel.

At the Vicarage there were no Smiths, though a daughter —with whom I was unhappily unable to get in touch—had come back to the town. Then I paid a tribute to old Mrs. Nash by looking at the house in which I had lodged with her, and after that I took a long walk in the lanes which I had tramped with Burras and Marks. Though the day was dull the little town was as placid and unspoilt as ever, but all about me was my youth of over forty years ago, and a poignancy such as I have rarely felt.

Chapter XV

THE LAST WORD

I DO not suppose I shall write again about Breckland, though
there is material enough and to spare. As it is I have written
six novels, but before I refer to them there is something that
I should make clear, and it is this. This is no subtle attempt
to publicize those books. I do not suppose I shall make
another penny out of one of them, for none—except perhaps
the first—is likely to be reprinted, and that one is capable of
standing on its own legs with no further help of mine.

That Breckland series was comprehensively planned, for
twelve novels were actually envisaged, though only six were
written. *God and the Rabbit* dealt with the fortunes of a village
family; *In this Valley* with Methodism and Radicalism; *This
String First* with a village shopkeeper; *The Questing Man* with
the returned soldier of the last war; *The Harvest is Past* with the
career of a farmer, and *July at Fritham* with a Breckland squire.
Those partly planned but never written were to be shaped
around the following central characters: a farm labourer, a
parson, an antique dealer, a doctor, a schoolmaster, and a
publican.

If those six books had ever been written, there would have
been little left of rural Breckland that was unrecorded, and
there the series would have ended. But the publishers had got
into financial difficulties, and then this war broke out and I
was at once called up for military service. But in spite of
those things I doubt if I should have finished that Breckland

series, unless some noble patron had seen fit to endow me.
The public was not interested in a remote corner of England
or the acts and occupations of its people, and though each
principal character was known to me, yet perhaps there must
also have been some deficiency in my powers of telling a story,
so that it failed to hold its own in competition against my
elders and betters in the pre-war period.

But those are not the reasons why I shall write no more
about Breckland. Those reasons are found in what I have
already written and in what I am about to write, and I would
prefer to give them no more categorically than that. And let
me reinforce or introduce them by a story.

A day or two ago my doctor paid a friendly call and found
me at work. I had just written that story that Wilson told
me of the half-witted son of old Tom who stole the carp, so
I told it to him. He in return gave me a story of personal
experience, and a pretty grim story it is.

In the last war and in a certain area of England there was
a medical man of considerable importance who was in charge
of malingerers and malingering, and it is indicative of the
character of this man that he took an enormous and almost a
sadistic pleasure in his job.

One morning he called at a certain hospital. He said he was
uncommonly busy and unless there was anything special he
would not go round the wards.

'I don't think there's any need,' the doctor on duty told
him. 'There's nothing unusual of any sort.'

'Then I'll be going,' the other said.

'No reason why you shouldn't,' he was told. 'But wait a
minute, though. There *is* that malingerer in the last bed in
Ward 5. But you wouldn't want to see *him*.'

The O.C. Malingerers pricked his ears.

'That chap, eh? And what little tricks has he been up to
now?'

'Oh, nothing particular,' the other told him. 'He just
happened to die last night—that's all.'

That story—or should we call it a parable?—may be grim
but it has an even grimmer application. For that malingerer
was the British farmer: that inter-war mixture of nuisance
and mountebank. The wireless portrayed him as part clown,
part die-hard. It gave him dialects that existed only in the

slick brains of its back-room programme boys, and the interests and aspirations of a clodhopper clown. How easy for the comedian to raise a laugh with talk of his muck-spreedin' time or 'Oi be in love with she', or his fat-stock prices. There were the farmer's grumblings, hoary as antiquity Never was the weather right for him and never did he get a fair deal and there was his perpetual cry of Wolf! when no wolf ever came. And then one morning the British public woke up to find that he was dead. The wolf of cheap imported food had killed him and he was dead as New Zealand mutton.

That he was resuscitated is no matter, nor are the repeated promises and vows that never again shall he get beyond the doctor's aid. For my corner of England is Heathley, and Heathley was past all help of doctors.

Now the paradox, and a grimly ironic one it is, is that for Heathley this last war came too late. Had it broken out as little ago as twenty years, not only might it have been saved but it must have become a community even more flourishing than when I first knew it fifty years ago. But let me make myself clear.

Modern methods of mass production would not have saved it, for it had no need of them. Nor would cheap and abundant fertilizers, for they would have been no more than temporary and unstable tonics for land as light as ours. What would have saved it was the fixing of reasonable prices for home-grown meat so that a man could rear and fatten stock. It is the old story of the bullock around which heath farming revolved. Wyatt could make farming pay when prices were at none too high a level. The dung from his bullocks enriched his land and kept it in heart, and the abundant corn his land grew had a fair home market.

But I see more to it than that. Modern methods which war needs have produced would have restored hundreds of our acres that the rabbit and pheasant had sent out of cultivation. There are methods of dealing with bracken that we never knew, and all those great areas that I was to live to see overrun might have had again the stacks that stood thick as the fingers of a hand. But the war, as I said, came too late. The serried plantations of the Forestry Commission stand where those stacks might have been, and on many a field that only twenty years ago was reasonably fertile land.

I am writing these words on VE Day, and I think of

Heathley as it will be. I know it will be making a brave
show, if only with the flags that hang from its cottage windows.
The last war took a score of its young men and this war will
have taken more, and those that still fight will be scattered
over the face of the earth. The spirit is there though thoughtlessness and facile exigency have killed its acres.

Perhaps all that is vaguely why I cannot write again about
Heathley. For me there is one Heathley—the village I knew
as a boy, and not that regimented attenuated thing at whose
outlying fields I am afraid to look. That lost Heathley is
what I have tried to perpetuate: its thriving communal life,
the kindliness of its common folk, the simplicity of its faith
and its customs that go back to time itself.

This simple book ends early in the century. It was just
after the last war that the inevitable changes came, to be
followed by those of men's making. Perhaps you would like
to know the subsequent history and the things that I lived to
see. There were, for instance, the gaps that I found after that
last war when at last I came home, and the many faces I was
never again to see. Both John Pardon and Squire Finch had
gone, and the village was under a New Dispensation of
Church and State. Green had gone, and in the Hall was no
tenant. Soon the shooting was to be let to a—what shall I
call them?—a collection of Newmarket jockeys and small
trainers. Once, owing to the shortage of men, I was asked to
let my gardener go brushing, but he flatly refused. He had
known the shooting-parties of the old days, and the manners
and fouler language of the new shooting tenants was something he and the village could never stomach.

Many of the old Methodists had gone, as had that notable
figure of my boyhood—Dodger Lake. Dodger had left the
village to accompany a Heathley farmer who had bought a
farm elsewhere, and, apt for an old poacher, he died with a
gun in his hand. But it was his own brains that he blew out,
and one morning they found him lying in a meadow. Field,
too, had left the village to follow Green, and his last days were
spent in drawing the invalid chair in which his master was
moved about. Green had promised him that he should never
want, and then when Green died it was found that he had
omitted to make provision in his will, and Field was left with
only his savings and the old age pension on which to live.
The war and the poverty of the estate had also killed the

first home mile of the Wortley Road. Every tree of any size had been felled each side along its length and that superb tracery of bough and leaf had gone for ever. When I saw that road again it was as if I was in some strange and yet vaguely familiar place. Even the Deal Row was more gapped though its trees had been spared, if only because their ancient twisted trunks had no commercial value.

At first there was to be a brief yet tremendous persistence of war prosperity with the farmer still the darling of a hungry nation. During that war unimaginable things had happened. I had known small farmers whose best britches, if any, were darned and I came back to find them driving smart cobs and traps, and boasting of monies in the banks. Some had even gone to other villages and had bought big farms. I saw one such farmer and his son one day soon after my return, and I went across a field to speak to them.

'Well, Alfred,' I said. 'You seem to have done pretty well for yourself.'

'I don't know,' he said. 'Think of all the jolly money what we lost in that there war.' He turned to his son for confirmation. 'Didn't we, boy? Lost no end, we did.'

That made nonsense, until he explained. Every kind of crop had made so much money that a man with many irons in the fire had simply not the time to attend to all the things that might have added to his bank balance. He instanced swedes, for which he could have got a fabulous price a sack if only he'd had the time to get them to market.

I saw pigs make three pounds a-piece off the sow, and common stock at that. A farming company bought up land at Brackford and issued a circular to prospective shareholders, quoting the gigantic profits that could be made. One thing in the circular that tickled or riled us at Heathley was a picture of a labourer standing in a field of oats—an excellent picture it was too—and so tall were the oats that the man's head could only just be seen. But we knew that man, and that when the photograph was taken, he had been made to kneel!

Then that ephemeral prosperity came to an end. One day it was there and the next, as at the end of the South Sea Bubble, it had gone. Almost before men could adapt themselves to the new conditions, the whole county was in the grip of the most colossal slump. Once bullocks ceased to pay, the end was in sight. Sugar-beet staved off complete disaster for a few last years, but so narrow was the margin of living and so small the remnants of capital, that one bad sugar-beet year was enough to bring the end. But the townsman still had his cheap meat and bread and butter, so may I be permitted to put to that townsman as simple a case as he can ever have heard. He may not believe me, but the facts are unquestionable.

The wages of an agricultural labourer had risen from twelve shillings a week to over three times that sum. Every farming cost had risen at least to twice its pre-war figure, and cattle foods were even higher. *But for his corn the farmer was getting pre-war price, and, in some cases, less.* No juggling with paper figures or facile economics can alter that. I was to see the time when a farmer could roughly calculate beforehand just what his *loss* must be on each acre of land he sowed. And—ironic comment—the sovereign had gone; that small golden thing that had been in the old-time hessian bag as a symbol of stability. And other things had gone or were going too, and they also were symbols. The glory of the Flower Show had gone, as had that annual Whit-Sunday parade of the Friendly Societies. An attempt was made to revive it, but so small and pathetic was it that it was as if men winced when they saw the thing it had become.

And what did Heathley get by way of recompense for all this? I do not know, unless it were that on Saturday evening it had the opportunity of going to Ouseland in a motor-coach of sorts to see the pictures. It even had its wireless sets, battery operated, and soon instead of the *Honeysuckle and the Bee*, the boys would be whistling the tunes and singing the emetic lyrics of Charing Cross Road and Tin Pan Alley. And the village had other excitements that combined pleasure with the prospect of easy money, for football pools were in full swing and football and other competitions in the papers. The village was even canvassed to wean it from the *Eastern Daily Press* to the illustrated and other delights of the flashier London dailies. And if you urge against that the improvement in the labourer's pay and his weekly half-holiday, I would say that such things—taking account of the rise in costs—were largely superficial. No matter what a man's condition may be if the time has come when he has no work. As for the real improvements in his lot, I doubt if they will ever come to a village so remote. The Heathley labourer has the same cottage as his father before him. He has no main

water and no electric light.   At night he has to turn out to
the same antiquated garden privy, and his meals are cooked
and his room warmed by coal whose price would once have
been thought almost that of gold itself.

And finally may I be permitted to add another and more
personal change, and for that I would ask you to look again
at that rough plan of Ouseland School on page 119.   I mentioned a certain Speech Day but you may be startled to hear
that it was in some ways the most miserable of my life.   I
had heard from time to time of enormous improvements at
Ouseland and on those rare occasions when I passed the
school I would catch a glimpse of new red buildings in what
had been my old playground.   But when I came to the school
that day I received a personal shock.   For my old school
had gone.

The original building was there and reverently maintained,
but now that ancient room where I had spent my schooldays
was only a library.   The desks at which we had sat were gone,
and the piano and the desks of the masters too.   Even the
ghosts of those with whom I worked and played had gone,
and nothing of them was left but their names on a memorial.

The old gymnasium had disappeared and in its place was
a—to me—huge building that was not only an up-to-date
gymnasium but a first-class concert hall.   Beyond what had
been our playground were modern chemical and physical
laboratories.   There was a perfectly equipped manual room,
and a geography room and a music room, and many class-
rooms, and other things that I have forgotten.   In a despairing
moment I induced my mentor—the charming and courteous
mayor of the ancient borough—to go with me to find the
scene of my fight with Bumper Sayer, but even that had been
swallowed up.

What then could I say when I stood on that strange platform?   All that I had intended to say went by the board, and
I had to extemporize except in the matter of that necessary
true appraisal of myself.   All I could do—and it seemed a debt
I owed to my contemporaries—was to enlarge on the theme
that even before Agamemnon there were great men.   And yet
I suppose I should have been glad at that march of progress,
and, against that background of nostalgia and vague depression, glad I was.   Glad that the scholarship boys of to-day
have behind them, shall I say, that superbity of equipment, that

keen and supremely qualified specialist staff and a head master to whom nothing is of moment but the good of his school. Glad, too, that under such conditions that school would turn out men better armed for a battle with life and more certain of becoming citizens who would render to the State services more fine than ours who had been their predecessors. And then suddenly I wondered. Even now I do not know.

But it might be as well to end on a different note, even if that note is still personal. Among the hackneyed plots of the world is that one now so much in favour—the village boy who makes good. With that plot are mixed various modern ingredients, as the revenge element, so that the successful hero is able to live himself in the house of that once tyrannical squire, to reward his few faithful friends and to tread his enemies beneath his feet. I have yet to qualify as one who has at least in that way made good, and maybe that is why I feel but a scant satisfaction when the whirligig of time itself has seen fit to bring its own revenges. Nor can I always savour the full ironies, for in them is always something of humour or tragedy.

There was, for instance, old Potter of whom in my boyish years I stood in so much dread and from whom my terrified feet would run when I was abroad at night on unlawful occupation. I have mentioned elsewhere how he lost his wits and would wander aimlessly about the village in his retirement. On one such day I heard a strange muttering in the meadow that lay beyond my bowling-green. There stood old Potter, face red and moist as ever, and he was peering through the hedge at the long flowered vista to the house. 'Yes, yes, yes, yes, yes,' he was saying monotonously to himself. And then a moment of sanity would make a variation. 'Yes, yes, yes, yes, yes. Where do he get his money?'

When John Pardon died and his family left the village, there was an auction and my father bought the famous wagonette. It had been that wagonette that Wakeley Sayer—still happily alive at a great age—had driven in the pride of livery and cockaded hat, but above all it was the wagonette in which the cricket team, with John Pardon himself and John Balfour, the scorer, would travel to a cricket match. But when I saw that wagonette in our barn, it was as if I saw an old friend with his pathetic tray of matches by the kerb, and when it fetched me from Wortley or Harford stations, I hated to ride in it.

Once as a very small boy I was standing with Tom Edwards watching from the lane a tennis-party in progress on the Vicarage lawn. All at once I turned to Tom and announced that one day I was going to have a tennis-court and play tennis, but so boasting and absurd was the remark that Tom made never a comment. But how could I feel an irony when the time came that the then vicar played on a tennis-court of mine? Or that I should play that mysterious game at which John Pardon used to practise on the open spaces of the Plains?

I lived to see the passing of William Cash. He had been in his later years a bitter enemy to me and mine, but how could I feel even a touch of pleasure at his going? Enmities are easily forgotten. Less easily forgotten are those evenings when we rode together from Wortley Station in his old pony-cart and how he would talk politics and village history and embellish the tellings with sly sarcasms and that dry humour that spoke the bitterness of his mind.

Then there was the boy who happened to go by chance into Topleigh church and afterwards wrote an article that John Balfour sent to the *Ouseland and Hareborough Times*. He at least could feel no irony but only a curious pride and a stranger humility when only last year, at the centenary of the old *Norfolk News*, he was requested by the Editor to contribute to its centenary number an article on the agricultural labourer of the Norfolk of a hundred years ago.

And lastly comes an irony at which I still chuckle whenever it comes back to me. It concerns the last war. Potter had retired and young policemen took his place. When war broke out there was one who was known to be something of a poacher.

But there was also the need for special constables in the parish, and the choice fell on three or four men of seriousness and standing, though in their younger days they had been poachers almost to a man. Consider then the situation that arose, and temptations that had not been known since the days of St. Anthony. Slowly the old Adam gained the upper hand and at last the old poachers let themselves go. And who could blame them? There they were, girded in all the authority of the State, and at liberty to go where they would: invested in fact, like Dionise de Montchensy, with the right of free warren. So they, and the policeman, had a glorious war. What a harrying of pheasants! What snaring of hares!

What netting of rabbits! Such an ironic glee seizes me that
I have to continue with Keats:

> *What mad pursuit! What struggles to escape!*
> *What pipes and timbrels! What wild ecstasy!*

When I got back to England and heard of that, I had to pay
a call on one of those special constables. When he told me of
his exploits the tears rolled down his cheeks.

'Bast! you owt to have sin us arter them jolly pheasants!
They got so darned scared we had to go into other parishes
to fetch 'em back. Rabbits? You never seed such loads as
we usta cart home o' nights. Never suffered from no food
shortage here, we didn't.'

Then he fetched something for me to see, and as I took
it he laughed again.

'And then they went and give me this here jolly medal!'

On that note of Heathley laughter it might be best to end.
You may not appreciate that particular irony, but I was an old
poacher and I had suffered under the Game laws. The man
who heard that story was the boy of many years before. Maybe
that boy was akin to the men who had poached deer and game
in the time of that Dionise de Montchensy and her charter.
Maybe those men were the serfs of Edric, who in their way
were poachers too. But that is far too ancient a history, and,
as I now remember it, it is also a full circle, for it is where
this book began.

PRINTED BY
JARROLD AND SONS LTD.
NORWICH